Men of Steam

Men of Steam

Railwaymen in Their Own Words

David Wragg

WHARNCLIFFE
TRANSPORT

First published in Great Britain in 2011 by
WHARNCLIFFE TRANSPORT
An imprint of
Pen & Sword Books Ltd
47 Church Street
Barnsley
South Yorkshire
S70 2AS

ISBN 978-1-84563-133-8

Typeset by Concept, Huddersfield, West Yorkshire
Printed and bound in England by the CPI UK

Pen & Sword Books Ltd incorporates the Imprints of Pen & Sword Aviation,
Pen & Sword Family History, Pen & Sword Maritime, Pen & Sword Military,
Pen & Sword Discovery, Wharncliffe Local History, Wharncliffe True Crime,
Wharncliffe Transport, Pen & Sword Select, Pen & Sword Military Classics,
Leo Cooper, The Praetorian Press, Remember When, Seaforth Publishing and
Frontline Publishing.

For a complete list of Pen & Sword titles please contact
PEN & SWORD BOOKS LIMITED
47 Church Street, Barnsley, South Yorkshire, S70 2AS, England
E-mail: enquiries@pen-and-sword.co.uk
Website: www.pen-and-sword.co.uk

Contents

Acknowledgments

Obviously I am grateful for all those who worked on the railways and recorded their experiences and impressions, without which we would not have had such vivid accounts of what life was like on the steam railway. On reading these accounts, one learns so much more about what life was like and what the job really entailed than in reading straightforward narrative in a conventional history.

Such records are immensely valuable, and so I am especially grateful for the vast resource kept in the archives, or 'Search Engine', at the National Railway Museum in York, which is an invaluable resource for the nation and a veritable treasure trove for those interested in historical research into our railways. Just one part of this is the collection of magazines produced by the old railway companies, mainly for their employees but, unlike many in-house staff newspapers or magazines today, these were also available for the interested outsider. Now, they are available to anyone who cares to contact the Search Engine at York.

Glossary

Atlantic – Steam locomotive with a 4-4-2 wheel configuration.

Banker – A locomotive that is placed at the end of a train to provide assistance, either in starting or in ascending a gradient. It would not normally be connected to the train which would leave it behind as speed was gained.

'Big Four' – The four companies created from more than a hundred on grouping of the main line railways in 1923. These were, in order of size, the London, Midland & Scottish Railway (LMS); London & North Eastern Railway (LNER); Great Western Railway (GWR); and the Southern Railway (SR).

Bogies – Railway carriages with bogies, a swivelling truck on which the carriage or wagon is mounted, meaning that they are longer and larger, and of course heavier than the early rigid four and six-wheelers.

Check – see permanent way check below.

Checked – A train stopped at signals, which would never be described as a 'stop' by railwaymen.

Cut-off – Quoted as a percentage, this is the point in the piston stroke at which steam supply to the cylinders is stopped by closing the admission valve. The cut-off is reduced as speed increases, so that a locomotive might start off at 75 or 80 per cent cut-off, but at full speed this could be 15 per cent. A 'cut-off' was also a new stretch of line reducing the distance between two towns.

cwt – Abbreviation for hundredweight, which is 112 lbs, a twentieth of a ton.

Diagram – The schedule for a locomotive or multiple unit during its day's work.

Down – A train or the line running from London, or in Scotland from Edinburgh. Some companies used their head office as the starting point, so that the Midland Railway had 'down' for trains and lines running from its head office at Derby. In south Wales, trains rang 'down' the valleys to the coast.

Fitted – Freight train with wagons having brakes.

Gauge-glass – A glass tube on the footplate panel in front of the driver showing the level of the water in the boiler, and often another on the front of the tender would show how much water was left.

Imbibing – A steam locomotive taking on water while stationary.

Interlocking frame – equipment within a railway signal box that ensures that signals and points are connected so that conflicting or dangerous movements cannot be arranged.

Junior – A railwayman under the age of twenty years.

Length – The stretch of track allocated to a gang of platelayers.

Light/light engine – A locomotive running on its own without carriages or wagons. The term has nothing to do with the weight of the locomotive.

Link – A combination of duties for a group of personnel qualified to perform them. Often these included a 'top' or 'first' link whose members received the highest rates of pay and were awarded the prestige express workings.

Motion – The connecting rods and other mechanisms linking the cylinder with the wheels. On a two cylinder locomotive, these were usually on the outside, but three and four cylinder locomotives or those with 'inside' cylinders had cylinders that were difficult to reach.

On time –During the period under review, a train was either on time or late, unlike today when a delay of five minutes is allowed as on time for short distance services, and ten minutes for longer distance services.

Pacific – Steam locomotive with a 4-6-2 wheel configuration.

Permanent way check or slack – A temporary speed limit due to a fault with the line or during engineering work.

Pick-up goods – The slowest of all the goods trains that would stop at every goods station or depot to pick up loaded wagons or to deliver wagons for unloading. At many stations, the 'pick-up' goods would have to do its own shunting, which could take time, especially as the guards van always had to be at the end of the train.

Pilot – A steam locomotive that provides extra power and is placed at the head of a train in front of the train locomotive. It is usually connected to the other locomotive and the train braking system. The

Midland Railway was notorious for having small locomotives, so many of its trains were double-headed – the leading locomotive being the pilot.

Post Office tube railway – An underground railway connecting the Post Office headquarters in St Martins-le-Grand with most of the major railway termini in London. It is no longer used.

Regulation – Control of trains within the system to ensure safety and timekeeping.

Regulator – This is the valve that regulates the flow of steam to the cylinders and in general terms serves the same function as the throttle on aircraft engines or the accelerator in a car.

Road – The track.

Rulley – A type of horse-drawn wagon.

Six-foot – The space between adjoining tracks on the GWR lines, which was wider than on other railways because the lines had been laid as broad gauge.

Stop – A scheduled call at a railway station or halt, but never at signals.

Stud – A collection of locomotives (they were 'iron horses', after all) dedicated to a particular service or group of services.

Unfitted – Freight train with wagons that do not have a continuous braking system and must be manually and individually hand braked on arriving at their destination. Braking en route was by the locomotive, which meant that such trains could never be very fast.

Up – A train or line running towards London, or in Scotland towards Edinburgh. The Midland Railway was an exception with trains and lines running up towards Derby, while in south Wales trains ran 'up' the valleys from the coast.

Working timetable – The timetable used by railwaymen, never by the public. The working timetable would include timing points other than calls at stations, and in some cases the schedule might be slightly tighter than shown in the public timetable to make an on time arrival more likely. On the Southern Railway between Brighton and London Victoria, the working timetable gave fifty-eight minutes while the public timetable allowed an hour for non-stop trains.

Introduction

Nothing has quite the same appeal as a steam railway, and today preserved lines attract not just the enthusiast, anxious to savour the sounds and the distinctive aroma of a steam railway, but the casual holidaymaker who probably couldn't tell the difference between a 'Pacific' and an 'Atlantic', and perhaps knows little or nothing of the history of the old railway companies.

The men who worked the steam locomotives and those who worked around them inherited a different world from today's electric and diesel-operated railways. The railways were not simply a job for life, but the job was their life and it could take a good part of it to work from being an engine cleaner to fireman to driver, and from working on a shunter to driving a famous named express. Fortunately, the railways were so big and operated on such a scale that they felt the need to share the experiences of different categories of staff with one another through their employee magazines, so a substantial volume of narrative exists with not just drivers but guards, carriage and wagon inspectors, signalmen and others writing about their work. Unlike contemporary company periodicals, even employees had to pay for the publications, usually being encouraged to take an annual subscription. This actually explains why never more than a minority of employees subscribed, although one would hope that many would have passed around their copy to their colleagues or workmates.

Attitudes differed considerably from those of today, although perhaps the *LMS Magazine* was the most forward looking with its emphasis on productivity and sales, as well as the personal accounts, even if ghosted to some extent, by a wide range of railwaymen. The LNER approach was similar, while both the Southern and the Great Western preferred to write about people's jobs, and in the latter case, one editor, who attempted to gain first-hand experience of the different jobs around the company, usually wrote in the third person.

Typical of the type of first-hand account is one that describes the feelings of a young fireman who had been working on a shunting locomotive suddenly being asked if he could fire an overnight express for the first time.

'Don't you get nervous. I'll put you right,' said Fred the driver.

'I paid extra special care to the work of preparing the engine, wondering all the time if I had forgotten anything ... My responsibility was to keep 250 lb of steam in the boiler of the Royal Scot engine; to ensure there was sufficient water in the boiler; to pick up water from the troughs; and to do several other little jobs while the driver worked the *Night Scot*, weighing 400 tons, from Euston to Carlisle in two hours and fifty-seven minutes ...'

Picking up water from the troughs was important, otherwise long distance expresses would be delayed while they stopped to replenish the locomotive's water, a process known as imbibing. To ensure that the right amount of water was forced into the tender depended on the locomotive running at speed, and the scoop had to be dropped just as the trough started and be up safely before the end, otherwise there was the very real danger of a high speed derailment. Without water troughs, a steam locomotive had to stop every eighty miles or so, and usually it was quicker to change locomotives than to wait while the tender was replenished. This is what happened on the Southern Railway's 'Atlantic Coast Express', running from Waterloo to a variety of destinations in North Devon and Cornwall on a line without water troughs. The train ran through Salisbury, eighty miles from London, and stopped to change locomotives at Wilton, just to the west, although of course, to the true railwayman, the train didn't stop but was simply 'checked'.

The fireman was also expected to help the driver by keeping a look out for signals, on the basis that two pairs of eyes were better than one. While signals were for the most part on what motorists would describe as the nearside, which was the side on which drivers sat on most, but not all, of Britain's railways, the fireman's watching was especially important when signals were mounted on overhead gantries or when crossing a busy junction.

These were hard times, with much of this book set during the long economic depression that occupied so much of the two decades between the two world wars. Even without this, these were hard times for railwaymen, working longer hours than today, and with much filth and manual labour, as we will see in the tunnel inspection. A fireman would have to move 2 or 3 tons of coal from the tender of a large locomotive to the firebox before being relieved. The driver may have had an easier job, but his seat was anything but comfortable, often without a back support and seldom with any cushioning, while steam locomotives at speed had a harsh ride.

In this book, typical stories include that of a passenger guard, infuriated by passengers saying farewell to friends holding the carriage doors open while he blew his whistle, or the frustrations of a goods agent (basically a salesman).

Apart from the change from steam to diesel or electric, the 'old' railway differed in other ways. Today, the railways really only care about trainload freight, but the 'old' railway also accommodated wagonload freight and less than wagonload freight, known as 'smalls' or 'sundries', and parcels as well. Trains could be chartered, for when the circus arrived in town, it was usually by train, with wagons that included horse boxes and even special wagons to accommodate elephants, which would parade through the town from the railway station to the circus showground. If one was moving a farm, a train would be chartered. On a less ambitious and more domestic basis, moving house was also dependent on the train, and the introduction of containers between the two world wars eased this process with the household effects transferred easily within the container from road vehicle, even in 1939 still often horse-drawn, to railway wagon, and then back again at the other end for final delivery. In between, the wagon would be shunted from one train to another for rarely would the previous home and the new home be on the same line.

While trains were of all sorts and differing kinds, they also included narrow gauge railways and light railways. Most people even then regarded narrow gauge railways as 'toy' railways, but most were built with a serious business purpose in mind. The Welsh narrow gauge railways included those used to carry slate in areas where building a standard gauge railway would have been prohibitive because of the topography of the country. Perhaps the one that attracted the epithet of 'toy railway' most was the Romney, Hythe & Dymchurch, running across the Kent marshes, because of its locomotives being small scale replicas of mainline engines, but that apart, it was built to a narrow gauge to extend passenger services across land that could only with difficulty and great expense be persuaded to take the weight of a full-sized locomotive. It was, of course, unusual in that it was built with passengers in mind for most of the other narrow gauge railways were built primarily for goods traffic.

Light railways could be narrow or standard gauge, but had simplified signalling and control arrangements to reduce the cost of construction and operation, and as a result had a 25 mph speed limit. Some ran along the roadside and had 'tram engines', built so that the unwary pedestrian would not fall under its wheels. Those brought up on the Reverend Awdry's 'Railway Stories' will recall not just the immortal 'Thomas the Tank Engine', but also 'Toby the Tram Engine'. The diversity of Britain's railways allowed this author and Great Western enthusiast a large palette from which to pull the component parts of his railway, set peacefully on the island of Sodor and dominated by the benign Fat Controller.

The railways had progressed to become large and sophisticated organisations by the period between the two world wars, when steam was in its heyday even though challenged by both diesel and electric propulsion. Some magazine articles drew attention to the benefits of dieselisation or electrification, while others maintained stoutly that there was plenty of scope for further development with steam, with high hopes held for high pressure steam, which were to be disappointed with a fatal accident on the LMS prototype and costly maintenance and poor reliability on the LNER example. Even so, as the records were set, many could claim with justification that steam was the advanced technology of the day.

Certainly, life had improved out of all recognition for the passenger. In an article celebrating the inauguration of the 'Silver Jubilee' express between London and Newcastle, the *London & North Eastern Railway Magazine* noted that it coincided with the 110th anniversary of the opening of the Stockton & Darlington Railway. On that railway, the first 'train consisted of twelve wagons of coal, one wagon of flour (on all of which passengers had seated themselves), one wagon carrying the surveyor and engineers, "six wagons filled with strangers", fourteen wagons conveying workmen, and the first railway passenger carriage called "Experiment" – described in its maker's bill as "one coach body fit up with a door at each end, glass frames to the window, a table and seats for the inside, top seats and steps". This strange assortment of rolling stock – then the latest thing in transport ever seen on this small planet – was hauled by George Stephenson's Locomotive

No. 1, now adorning Darlington station, as the breath-taking speed of 8 miles per hour.'

The magazine continued to point out that the 'Silver Jubilee' was booked to run at an average speed of 72 mph between London and Grantham, while between Darlington and London the average of 70.3 mph was the fastest timing in the world for a run exceeding 200 miles.

All in all, much of the material here predates and even anticipates the 'Life in the Day of ...' features of the colour supplements of latter years. I wonder how useful these current day features will be in another sixty or seventy years?

Chapter 1

On the Footplate

Clearly, the glamour of engine driving was with those on the great expresses, and these men would be in what was known as the 'top link' of the engine shed or, in later years, motive power depot to which they were assigned. The link system provided a means of progression from driving a shunting locomotive through goods and stopping trains to semi-fast trains and then on to the expresses. A driver on the top link would be at the height of his profession, although he could be promoted to footplate inspector, the lower rung of operational management. Firemen also progressed through the same system, and then down again once promoted to driver.

This glamour meant that over many years others, including railway journalists and authors, sought permission to ride on the footplate. This seems to have been granted reasonably freely judging by the number of accounts that were published, mainly in the railway press. These 'observers' sometimes were very experienced and knew a great deal about the railway, but others were less well-informed. Often they would be accompanied by a footplate inspector, but not always. They do seem to have been made welcome by the locomotive crews, the footplatemen as they were known collectively, no doubt as a break from routine and also because they appreciated being picked out to look after a visitor. No doubt they also looked forward to seeing the account being published in due course.

Riding on the Footplate of *Tangmere*

The Southern Railway was the leading British proponent of electrification, giving London Europe's largest electrified suburban network, and then starting main line electrification, initially to Brighton and the Sussex coast, and then to Portsmouth, so that by 1938, that city had two electrified lines connecting it to London. Despite having some excellent steam locomotives, such as the Schools-class, which was the most powerful 4-4-0 of its day, the Southern lacked the Pacific locomotives that it really needed until the Second World War, when Oliver Bulleid introduced his Merchant Navy-class. These were known as 'spam cans' because of their squared-off boiler casing, which Bulleid himself described as 'air-smoothed'. They provided a comfortable working environment for the footplatemen, and although their unusual running gear meant that they could suffer severe failures, they were also flexible, and had to be as in order to build them during wartime austerity Bulleid had convinced the authorities that they were mixed traffic locomotives, not the express engines that they really were. The original Merchant Navy locomotives were too heavy for many lines, including those in Southampton Docks used by the boat trains. To serve the other non-electrified lines, Bulleid introduced lighter-weight versions in the West Country-class and the Battle of Britain-class, incorporating the features and shape of the Merchant Navy-class.

In this case we have Ransome-Wallis on the footplate, but this time as an observer, on the Battle of Britain-class locomotive *Tangmere*, named after a wartime RAF fighter station. He joined her at Ramsgate where she was waiting to take the 7.20am to Cannon Street. On a cold and frosty morning, with some fog in places, he found the cab to warm and clean.

> There was a fairly heavy fire, banked up well under the fire-hole door. 'Soon shakes down when we get going', said Williams [the fireman]. The pressure showed 250-lb on the gauge, and the water was well up in the glass.

He was impressed with the layout of the controls and a number of labour-saving features such as a steam-powered butterfly firedoor operated by a foot pedal. The one feature that jarred with him was the position of the vacuum brake ejector in front of the driver as this obstructed the look-out, especially for shorter drivers.

> Sharp at 7.20 we slid gently out of Ramsgate Station with a load of nine bogies and a restaurant car – forty axles and weighing about 320 tons. Dumpton Park, Broadstairs and Margate: station time was under two minutes at Margate and under a minute at each of the preceding stops. Boiler pressure had risen to blowing-off point on several occasions, the gauge reading varying between 260-lb and 275-lb when the valves lifted, and firing up to now had been light, with coal of moderate quality.

Leaving Margate, we began our first spell of fast running, for the eleven and a quarter miles to Herne Bay are allowed only fifteen minutes start to stop, and high speeds are impossible until Westgate is cleared, owing to the curvature of the road. We got away without any slipping, and with the regulator half-open and 30 per cent cut-off we maintained a steady 45 mph rising to 53 mph at Birchington. Ahead of us lay the straight and level road across the marshes ... a sustained 68½ mph and a nice run at the two miles of 1 in 100 up before the descent to Herne Bay ... took us over the top at 53 mph ... to coast down the bank the other side. Herne Bay distant was sighted at danger, for we were by this time two minutes ahead of schedule, but a long wail from our whistle and the signal cleared ... we came to rest in the station in thirteen minutes and twenty-five seconds from Margate.

Ransome-Wallis continued to note that the tenders of the loco-motives were small due to the length of the turntables on the Southern, so they could carry just 5 tons of coal and 4,500 gallons of water. The water capacity was increased on later versions.

Tangmere reached her last booked stop before London, Whitstable, on time, but poor station work meant that she left twenty seconds late. Nevertheless, *Tangmere* then had the benefit of straight track over Greveney Marshes, reaching 62 mph before dropping to 40 mph to cross the junction at Faversham, after which a series of rising gradients kept the speed to around 50 mph. As they approached the Medway towns, fog descended, and a series of signal checks as they ran through Chatham soon meant that they were running three minutes late as they approached Sole Street Bank, a rising gradient of 1 in 100 for five miles.

The bank is approached from this direction by a severe curve which is a hindrance to trains coming down the bank, but an absolute curse for trains going up. A run at the bank is impossible and locomotive work of a very high order is necessary to maintain schedule ... with the light axle load of the ... class very careful driving is called for if slipping is to be avoided. *Tangmere* was doing 35 mph exactly, as we came out of the curve and set about the bank. The damp cold air had made the rails very greasy and Clapson (the driver) opened up his sanding gear before he attached the bank in earnest. The regulator was gently opened from half to three-quarters, and cut-off brought back from 20 per cent to 30 per cent. With boiler pressure at 240-lb this now gave us 210-lb in the steam chest and a steady speed of 33 mph with a momentary increase to nearly 35 mph at the short level stretch in the middle of the bank. The fog had cleared by now ... and we passed Sole Street Station two minutes and forty seconds late, but with only 190-lb steam in the boiler. However, we now got going to some purpose and by Fawkham we touched 69 mph and 79 mph at Farningham Road ... We passed Chislehurst at 9.04 exactly – right time – regained the time lost at Chatham. Then fog came down with a vengeance and fogmen were out as we crawled through Hither Green with nothing more encouraging than a double yellow. I must give credit to the Southern colour light signals. They are perfectly sighted and they pierce the fog to an amazing extent. From the footplate there is never any doubt about which is yours ... In spite of the murk we kept moving and Borough Garden Junction gave us a clear road for the right-hand fork into Cannon Street. So we came to rest at 9.25, or five minutes and fifty-eight seconds late by my chronometer.

Ransome-Wallis noted that Williams, the fireman, had been shovelling at eight to ten shovels at a time, placing the coal in three positions only, under the firedoor and in each back corner. The coal shook down evenly with the motion of the engine.

The locomotive would not necessarily have worked back from Cannon Street, a station that was only ever really busy during the rush hours, but after refuelling and watering at a sub depot between Cannon Street and Charing Cross, would have worked a late morning train possibly from Charing Cross to Ramsgate via Folkestone, Dover and Deal, making a circuit of Kent.

It is perhaps worth mentioning that office workers, and especially those in the City of London, worked much shorter hours in 1946 than today. A 9.30am or even a 10.00am start was not unusual, and most would be away by 5.00 or 5.30pm.

On the 'Flying Scotsman'

The 'Flying Scotsman' refers to the train, not the locomotive, and in fact while a number of the locomotive was recorded (No. 2582 from Newcastle shed), strangely the name was not, although it seems that it was the A3 Pacific *Sir Hugo*. The article comes from the *London & North Eastern Railway Magazine* and was written by Eric Gill.

Unusually, the beginning of the piece is garbled, seemingly Gill being introduced to the engine driver, a Mr Young, twice:

I was born beside the railway at Brighton, and spent most of my childhood examining and drawing locomotives, and what surprised me now was, first, how little things had changed in fundamentals since I was a child thirty-five years ago and, second, how simple in idea the mechanism of steam engines still is. A detail that struck me immediately was that the throttle lever on the LNER engine was worked by pulling it upwards towards you, whereas on the engines of my Brighton childhood it was worked by a lever at right angles to the axis of the boiler.

The remaining few minutes were spent in explanations of the brake apparatus, steam pressure required – the names of this and that and then someone called up from outside: 'right you are' and I gathered that it must be exactly 10.00. The engine was driven from the right hand side, so I was given the piano-stool or perch on the left side, with one foot on a pail (a quite ordinary house-hold looking pail) and the other dangling. Up to this time, the fireman had been doing various odd jobs about the place. He now shut (if you can call it shutting, for it only about half covered the gap) the iron door between engine and tender, and Mr Young, having made a suitable response to the man outside who had shouted 'right you are,' pulled up the handle (both hands to the job and not too much at a time – a mouthful, so to say, for a start, to let her feel the weight) and, well, we simply started forward. It's as simply as that. I mean it *looks* as simple as that.

And immediately, the fireman started shovelling coal. I shouted some apology to him for taking his seat. I could not hear his reply. It was probably to say that he had no time for seats. He shovelled in about six shovelsful; and then after a few seconds pause, another half-dozen – a few seconds pause and then six or more shovels and so on practically without stopping the whole time. What strikes you about this, even more than the colossal labour of the thing and the great skill with which he distributes the coal in the fire and his unerring aim in throwing a pretty big shovelful of coal through a not very large opening, what strikes you is the extraordinary primitive nature of the job. You stand in a space about as big as a hearth rug spread out longways to the fire and you take a shovel of coal out of a hole at one end and throw it through a hole in the other end – spilling a bit every time. You go on doing this for hours. Your attention must be as great as your skill and strength. You must watch the pressure gauges and you must watch the state of the fire at the same time. And your only relaxations are when, on entering tunnels or passing stations, you give a tug at the whistle handle and when, on a signal from the driver, you let down the water scoop to take up water from the trough between the rails (which occurs every hundred miles or so). And talking of primitive things, look at the whistle handle! It is a round ring on the end of a wire (there is one on each side of the cab). It dangles down about a foot from the roof. When the train is travelling fast you have to make a bit of a grab for it as it is never in the same place for two seconds together. On receiving a nod of acquiescence from Mr Young, I pulled the handle myself as we approached Peterborough, and again as we went, at reduced speed, through the station itself. (My first pull was but a timid little shriek, but my second was, it seemed to me, a long bold blast.)

But don't imagine I'm complaining or sneering about this primitiveness. It's no more primitive or less venerable than sawing with a hand saw or ploughing with a horse plough. I only think that it's surprising how these primitive methods persist. He we were on an engine of the most powerful kind in the world, attached to one of the most famous of all travelling hotels – the string of coaches called 'The Flying Scotsman' – with its cocktail bar and beauty parlours, its dining saloons, decorated in more or less creditable imitations of the salons of eighteenth-century France, its waiters and guards and attendants of all sorts, its ventilation and heating apparatus as efficient as those of the Strand Palace Hotel, and here we were carrying on as if we pulling a string of coal trucks.

All the luxury and culture of the world depends ultimately on the efforts of the labourer. This fact has often been described in books. It has also been the subject of cartoons and pictures – the sweating labourer groaning beneath the weight of all the arts and sciences, the pomps and prides of the world – but here it was in plain daily life.

And what made it even more obvious was the complete absence of connection with the train behind us. The train was there – you could see it if you looked out when going round a bend – but that was all. And just as the passenger very seldom thinks about the men on the engine, so we thought nothing at all about the passengers. They were simply part of the load. Indeed there may not have been any passengers – we weren't aware of any.

And the absence of connection between engine and train was emphasised by the entirely different physical sensations which engine travelling gives you. The noise if different – you never for a moment cease to hear, and to feel, the effort of the pistons. The shriek of the whistle splits your ears, a hundred other noises drown any attempt at conversation.

Though the engine is well sprung, there is also a feeling of hard contact on the rails all the time – something like riding on an enormously heavy solid-tyred bicycle. And that rhythmic tune which you hear when travelling in the train, the rhythm of the wheels as they go over the joints in the metals (iddy UMty ... iddy UMty ... &c.) is entirely absent. There is simply a continuous iddyiddyiddy ... there is sensation of travelling *in* a train – you are travelling *on* an engine. You are on top of an extremely heavy cart horse which is discharging its terrific pent-up energy by the innumerable outbursts of its breath.

And continuously the fireman works, and continuously the driver, one hand on the throttle lever, the other ready near the brake handle (a handle no bigger than that of a bicycle and yet controlling power sufficient to pull up a train weighing 500 tons) keeps watch on the line ahead for a possible adverse signal. If the signals are down, they go straight ahead, slowing down only for the sharper curves and the bigger railway junctions. You place absolute trust in the organisation of the line and you know practically every yard of it by sight. You dash roaring into the small black hole of a tunnel (the impression you get is that it's a marvel you don't miss it sometimes) and when you are in you can see nothing at all. Does that make you slow up? Not at all – not by half a mile per hour. The signal was down; there can't be anything in the way and it's the same at night. I came back on the engine from

Grantham in the evening, simply to find out what they *can* see. You can see nothing but the signals – you know your whereabouts simply by memory. As for the signals; it's surprising how little the green lights show up compared with the red. It seemed to me that they went more by the absence of a red light (in the expected place) than by the presence of a green one. You can see the red miles away but the green only when you are almost on it. And if it seemed a foolhardy proceeding to rush headlong into tunnels in the day time, how much more foolhardy did it seem at night to career along at 80 miles an hour in a black world with nothing to help you but your memory of the road and a lot of flickering lights – lights often obliterated by smoke and rain. And here's another primitive thing: You can generally see nothing at all through the glass windows of the cab at night because the reflections of the firelight make it impossible. To see the road, to see the signals, you must put your head out at the side – weather or no. The narrow glass screen prevents your eyes from being filled with smoke and cinders, but, well, it seems a Garden of Eden sort of arrangement all the same.

And they don't even fill the tender with coal of the required size. Sometimes a big lump gets wedged into the opening and it has to be slowly broken up with a pickaxe before it can be dis-lodged – what about that? Well, I call it jolly fine; but it's jolly rum too, when you think of all the electric gadgets and labour-saving contrivances which the modern housewife thinks herself a martyr if she doesn't get. Up the long bank before Grantham – yes, and you notice the ups and downs when you're on the engine. They are both visible and hearable. You hear the engine's struggle (there's no 'changing down' when it starts 'labouring'). You feel it too, and, looking straight ahead, and not only sideways like the millionaire in the train behind you, you see the horizon of the bank before you. It *looks* like a hill. And when you run over the brow you *see* the run down and you hear the engine's change of breath, you hear and feel the more easy thrust of the pistons.

And, on the return journey, going down into London in the dark (on No. 2750 [the A3 locomotive *Papyrus*], with Mr Guttridge and Mr Rayner, a London engine and London men) with steam shut off and fire nearly out – just enough fire to get home with – we were pulled up by an adverse signal. Good that was too.

Nothing visible in the darkness but the red lights above our heads. Silence during which the fireman told me that Mr Guttridge had driven the King 28 times. Suddenly, one of the red lights turned green – sort of magical. 'Right ho,' said the fireman.

Sir William Stanier from Euston to Carlisle

Instead of a commuter express, Ransome-Wallis also chose a long distance express on the West Coast main line for another footplate ride. Interestingly, he was not concerned so much with a comparison between the Southern Railway and the London Midland & Scottish, but between the latter and the New York Central. He points out that while the NYC line is level compared with the heavily graded WCML, the loading of trains on the latter route was seldom half the tonnage hauled by the NYC's J-3 Hudsons. Another point of difference was that the American locomotives had mechanical stoking, while the British locomotive was hand-fired. The American locomotives had vastly superior boiler power, although tractive effort was, according to R.-W., roughly the same.

His locomotive was one of the last built by the LMS before national-isation, No. 6526, appropriately named *Sir William Stanier FRS*. Disap-pointment on joining the locomotive was caused by the realisation that, by LMS standards, the load was a light one, with just twelve carriages weighing 360 tons, or about 390 tons fully loaded, compared to the 800 tons of the 'Empire State Express' of the NYC. Small wonder the driver told him that, 'She'll play with this lot.'

Out of Euston there is the mile-long bank up to Camden, 1 in 70 at its steepest part; with a 'cold' engine this can be a source of trouble for the rest of the journey, for if the engine is worked too hard it will upset the fire, and this may influence the steaming of the boiler for a long time after. Our driver opened the regulator to one-quarter, and with help from the banking engine at the rear we quietly and rapidly got away. Full cut-off was used only until we had got the train away from the platform, after which the regu-lator was opened up to one-third, and then to a little more than half, while the reversing gear was brought back to 45 per cent, and then to 30 per cent. Finally, we passed Camden No. 1 Box at the top of the bank, in one second over three-and-a-half minutes. The engine was now notched up to 20 per cent cut-off, while the regulator remained just over half open. With the exhaust from our double blast pipe almost inaudible we accelerated easily and passed Willesden in nine-and-three-quarter minutes and Watford in twenty-two and three quarter minutes from the start.

The engine was steaming well at this time, and the exhaust was going well over the top of the cab despite the easy running. With the controls unchanged we went sailing up the long easy climb to Tring summit which was passed at 60 mph exactly, and we were through the station, thirty-one and three-quarter miles from Euston, in three seconds under thirty-seven minutes ... The driver now came over to me and shouted, 'We're all right, we shall be right time at Rugby, but she'll roll a bit!' The engine seemed to echo these ideas and went rolling happily down the gradual descent to Leighton Buzzard, with a maximum of 71 mph through Cheddington.

Into the single bore of Linslade Tunnel we went at 67 mph, covering our faces to avoid the whirling coal dust, and then out into the pleasant Buckinghamshire countryside ... our speed remained almost constant to Wolverton, and we were soon picking up water from Castlethorpe troughs before climbing again to Roade. On this climb of nearly seven miles with a ruling gradient of 1 in 326, I was surprised that the controls still remained as they had been since Tring summit and, as indeed, they were to be until shutting off for Rugby. Down the hill from Roade to Blisworth speed rose to 66 mph and did not fall below 60 mph until we topped the rise to Kilsby Tunnel at 58 mph. Kilsby Tunnel is a little over a mile and one-third long, and has two large ventilating shafts as well as a number of smaller ones. The glow of vivid orange-red light from these shafts appearing through the swirling smoke and darkness of the tunnel was weird and frightening, and I wondered how Dante would have interpreted the scene.

Apart from the necessarily hard firing on Camden bank, the locomotive performed easily with between twelve and fifteen shovels at a time every eight to ten minutes, with the coal placed mainly under the firedoor and in the back corners, with the boiler pressure maintained between 230 and 250-lbs. Rugby was reached on time despite a five minute late start from Euston, having taken eighty-eight minutes for the eighty-two and a half miles, giving an average of just under 56 mph throughout. At Rugby, a station dwell time of four minutes was stretched to six, so the train was again late as it departed for Crewe with a new driver and fireman. R.-W. was on a new locomotive with good quality control, in contrast to the usual post-war situation of poor maintenance, a hang-over from the pressures of the war years, and poor quality coal, but the run from Rugby to Crewe had no severe gradients and with ninety-three minutes to cover seventy-five and a half miles, getting back on time was not difficult. The one problem was a 20 mph permanent way check, presumable due to track maintenance, of almost a mile through Nuneaton, but after this speeds as high as 77 mph were achieved and the locomotive arrived with its train eight minutes early. On taking over, the driver had remarked to R.-W. that he 'didn't often have these engines', it seems that he certainly knew how to handle them. The one problem was that either through the inexperience of the fireman or sooting up of the tubes, steaming was difficult.

The extra time spent at Crewe due to the early arrival was welcome, as R.-W. had to refill his water bottle which was much resorted to on a hot summer day, and also grab a quick snack and a drink.

North of Crewe, the line became far more demanding, with many steep gradients between the town and Carlisle, including the steep ascent and descent at Shap, and in addition subsidence caused by coal mining also meant that there were many speed restrictions. In fact, the section between Crewe and Preston saw one speed restriction after another, sometimes down to 40 mph but in other cases even lower, with a limit of 20 mph. Even so, the driver was able to reassure R.-W. that they would Crewe 'on time, or bust!'

We got the green flag at 4.14pm, on time, and we went away gently from Crewe. Clattering over the complicated system of points and crossing at Crewe North Junction. Speed was soon worked up to a level mile-a- minute, but we were checked to 40 mph through Warrington, and got distant signals against at Wigan ... The engine was now opened up and, observing carefully the 15 mph restriction at Boars Head (where the station buildings have subsided so far that the window-sills are level with the platform!), we roared up to Standish with terrific vigour, passing the summit at 42 mph. Down the other side we ran until brought to a dead stand outside Preston while a leisurely freight went across our path. 'Tubby' (the driver) smiled and said: 'Can't really blame him – we're five minutes early.'

After standing for forty seconds, we were away once more, passing slowly through Preston station at 5.23, two minutes early. The boiler thus far had steamed rather better and, apart from a short period when 200-lb only was on the gauge, the pressure had not fallen below 220-lb.

The next twenty-one miles to Lancaster are booked to be covered in twenty-two minutes over what is virtually a level road, and after getting away from Preston we soon settled down to a steady rate of 65 mph. In spite of the fact that this was achieved with no more than one-quarter regulator opening and 15 per cent cut-off, the boiler pressure continued to fall and the crew were getting a little anxious about the thirty miles of climbing to Shap, summit, which really starts after Carnforth. To add to our troubles we were checked by distant signals before Lancaster, which was passed on time, in spite of taking twenty-four minutes from Preston (where we had been two minutes early). Another bad check to a walking pace at Morecambe South Junction did not improve matters, but the fireman had now got 210-lb on the gauge and we swept through Carnforth at 66 mph. The regulator was opened up to one half and with 20 per cent cut-off speed dropped to a minimum of 42 mph before Oxenholme was passed, nearly three minutes early ... On up to Grayrigg, with the lovely mountains of the Lake District looking kindly and soft ... But on turning my gaze from this lovely view to the more mundane dial of our pressure gauge, things were nothing like so lovely: pressure was down to 165 lb ... we were going up the bank quietly and easily and passed Grayrigg at 30 mph. Once over the top of the bank ... achieved 62 mph through Low Gill and 65 mph before slowing down drastically before Tebay. An under-bridge just south of Tebay station was being repaired and a speed restriction of 5 mph was in force ... not only were we denied the flying start on the climb to Shap – you usually get half-way up before the need to extend the engine is felt – but we were also denied the impetus necessary for No. 6256 to fill her tender from Dillicar water troughs just south of Tebay.

Secretly, I was delighted. Here, at any rate, was a chance to see what the engine would really do, if only the boiler would steam;

the 175-lb on the gauge was certainly not reassuring. However, with three-quarter regulator and 30 per cent cut-off the engine sounded quite businesslike as cleared Tebay Station, and soon after the cut-off was increased to 35 per cent, which took us to Scout Green Box, passed at 23 mph with 180-lb on the gauge. 'Tubby' looked relieved at our progress so far … he opened the regulator to full … and, as he described it later, 'she did cough a bit'. Speed was now 22 mph and there it stayed as we curved gently round to the summit, past the old platelayer's hut where so often I have sheltered from the rain when photographing on the bank. We passed the summit at 6.43½pm, only a minute and a half behind time, and still had 175-lb pressure in the boiler. Away we went like the wind, winding our way round the curves to Penrith at a maximum of 75 mph. A raucous shriek from the whistle and braking gently to 50 mph we swept through the curve of Penrith station. On under clear signals to Carlisle, we ran in at 7.13pm exactly – four minutes early. After six and a quarter hours of hot, hard riding I left the footplate, while No. 6256 went to Upperby shed to prepare for a south-bound trip later that night.

As he went to his hotel, R.-W. reflected that the locomotive had done well and had often been ahead of time, but he regretted that he had not seen her loaded to 500 tons and being really extended as she attempted to maintain pre-war schedules, which were much tighter and more demanding than those on the post-war railway. Even so, The NYC Hudsons would have been running at 80 mph with an 800-ton train.

Riding the 'Black Five'

One of the most popular classes of steam locomotives from the time they first appeared in 1934 were Sir William Stanier's Class 5s, or 'Black Fives', a highly capable and successful 4-6-0 mixed traffic loco-motive that has survived into preservation in greater numbers than any other type. The need for the type was such that Stanier gave it priority when he first joined the London Midland & Scottish from the Great Western, and in its design one can see many GWR features, including the tapered boiler and the 4-6-0 wheel arrangement.

Once again Ransome-Wallis managed to get official approval for a ride on the footplate. What makes this particular journey so interesting is that this was a goods train, something that the LMS and the GWR would both have referred to as a freight train, while most accounts from the cab have been on express locomotives often heading the famous named expresses. The date is not given, but it is almost certain that this was during the late 1940s, and although two mainline diesels are mentioned the fact that he writes 'the two main-line diesels' suggests these were the two ordered by the LMS before nationalisation, with one delivered in late 1947 and the other after nationalisation. The locomotive was clearly still suffering from the post-war backlog of maintenance as R.-W. came across the engine sitting in the shed at Carlisle, filthy and deserted, with black smoke coming from her chimney as she awaited her crew to sign on. What we do know is that the locomotive, No. 45106, renumbered by British Railways, was set to work the 6.50am freight from Carlisle's Upperby Yard to Crewe, where she was scheduled to arrive at 2.20pm, and that one reason for his being put on the train was that this departure was usually punctual.

One of the big differences between freight and passenger working was that passenger trains usually had their weight given in tons, but instead he was told that the train consisted of '41 equal to 51', meaning that several of the goods wagons were not the usual four-wheeled type but six-wheeled, or even eight-wheeled and with bogies. The first six were 'piped', which means that they were 'fitted', in other words they had vacuum brakes, so that the train was partially-fitted. He was not able to ascertain the weight of the train.

The locomotive had just over a hundred pounds of steam on the gauge when he boarded, but by the time the crew had joined, the water tank replenished and the locomotive backed on to her train, this had risen to 200-lbs, not far short of the locomotive's 225-lb upper limit. Even so, departure was at 7.07am, seventeen minutes late, with the train easing itself out of the yard and on to the main line, with the regulator nearly fully open and 35 per cent cut-off. The train soon settled down to a speed of between 30 and 36 mph. At Penrith, the train stopped for more water and an examination of the wagons, when it was found that two bogie wagons carrying machinery near the back of the train had trouble, and when the train was diverted into a passing loop, R.-W. suspected that they might have to be left behind. Had they done so, some shunting would have been required as at the time all goods trains had to have the guards van at the end of the train for safety reasons. A train examiner, the guard and the yard foreman conferred, and eventually whatever was the wrong was remedied and the train was clear to go. But by this time it was forty-five minutes late and the chances of a good through run to Crewe were doubtful.

At last we were 'Right Away' for Shap, and with 50 per cent cut-off and the regulator about three-quarters open, we made a good climb of the northern approach to the summit without speed falling below 20 mph. After a ten-minute wait in the loop at the summit, to let a southbound express go by, we were off again – coasting gently down the bank with the pleasant smell of hay coming up to us from this lovely countryside. Seldom have I seen Shap look so beautiful, basking in the morning sunshine ...

At Carnforth came another stop for water and examination of the train, and here the engine crew was changed. Sixteen minutes and we went again, this time with a stocky little Lancashire driver and a young and rather discontented fireman. However, they were good company and before they left the engine had plenty of time to talk. As far as Lancaster all went well, but after that the trouble started. Due to our early delays, we had lost our path in the timetable and we were now 'nobody's baby'. From Lancaster to Preston – twenty-one miles – took and hour and forty-one minutes, and after getting a fairly good road to Standish, we were put on the Wigan avoiding line ('the back road') and soon came to rest in the open country about five miles from Bamfurlong Junction. Here we sat in the full glare of the midday sun for over an hour and a half. It gave me a good opportunity to discuss all manner of things with the men. At that time the threat of a 'go-slow' was very real. Our driver would have none of it; he was quite contented with his lot, although he was obviously and clearly wishing that the days of the old North-Western were back again. He always, he said, had got along very nicely and he was disgusted at the state of the engines (which he loved) to-day. And, in those days, you knew who everybody was – a sort of family atmosphere – it was all too impersonal to-day. And so he talked on, with many happy stories of engines and men, both good and bad.

The young fireman was in a quandary; he liked railroading, but he also wanted to get married. There was a good job going at the local outfitter's shop – six pounds ten a week, regular hours, and 'you kept your hands clean'. On the present job he never knew quite how much he would take home. It was usually less than the outfitter offered, and you were away all hours of the day and night. I tried to point out to him that this was a man's job, that any girl could serve behind a counter; yes, he agreed he loved engines – always had done – but his wife-to-be had decided views in the other direction. I would like to know what his decision was, but I feel that the railway lost a good youngster and that a young wife and a pair of clean hands won the day. It seemed a great shame that there should be more money in selling shirts.

Ultimately, the signal dropped and we started away once more. Back on the main line, and with another engine crew, we continued our halting journey southwards. Nine more signal stops – at one place we became a 'pick-up' goods, as the local freight was running hours behind us, and at 6.45pm we ran into Crewe. Twelve hours on the footplate was, I thought, something of a feat of endurance ...

This had been a complete contrast to his other experiences on the fast expresses, and on a train that had to give way to them, entering passing loops so that the faster trains could continue unchecked.

The 'North Atlantic Express'

On the eve of the Second World War, Ransome-Wallis found himself in Northern Ireland with the opportunity to travel on the Northern Counties Committee's line from Belfast to Portrush, itself a branch off the main line to Londonderry. This was part of the sprawling London Midland & Scottish Railway's empire, inherited from the Midland Railway which had acquired the Belfast & Northern Counties Railway.

The 'North Atlantic Express' was booked to cover the sixty-five miles from Belfast to Portrush in eighty minutes, but on Saturdays, when there was a much heavier load, the time was reduced to seventy-seven minutes, including the one booked stop at Ballymena. This was the fastest run in the island at that time. Through the courtesy of Major Malcolm Speir I was able to travel on the footplate of the engine working this Saturday train, and I joined the engine at York Road Station, Belfast. The train was made up to nine bogies and the engine was No. 95 *The Braid*, running at that time with a jumper blast pipe and wide chimney (the only one of the series). It was also the only engine to have a Caledonian hooter instead of the usual high-pitched peanut whistle. The driver was very apologetic, for it transpired that his regular engine was having a boiler washout and this was a spare one that was due for the shops very soon, and he was afraid we might have rather a rough ride. How right he was! I have never been on a rougher engine, and by the time we reached Portrush I ached in every limb. But how these 6-foot engines can run, and how well the boiler steamed, despite the general run-down condition of the engine! Full regulator was used throughout, with cut-off as early as 15 per cent for much of the way, and despite a dead stand for signals for forty-five seconds outside Ballymena we went into that station on time – thirty-four minutes for thirty-one miles, or about thirty-one and a half minutes net.

We had a clear road after that and had no difficulty getting into Portrush half a minute early. Over the single line sections the automatic tablet catcher was brought into use, but speed did not have to be greatly reduced, the facing points into the passing loops being beautifully aligned ... I came back to Belfast on another 2-6-0 No. 97 *Earl of Ulster*. Although the up-train was much slower, and stopped at Coleraine, Ballymena and Antrim, we made some very smart running. No. 97 was in very smart condition and the contrast in the riding of the two engines was most marked. I had never realised quite what a difference there could be in the riding of two engines – one ready for the shops and one recently out.

Ransome-Wallis continued by mentioning a post-war visit to Ireland and to bemoan the end of the NCC and the arrival of the Ulster Transport Authority, the Northern Irish equivalent of the British Transport Commission. He also ventured south of the border, but without further footplate rides.

Chapter 2

In the Station

While there were very many unmanned halts in the remoter corners
of the railway network, even on some of the main lines, most towns
and many villages had at least one station. Frequently, in a larger town
there would be several and it was important to avoid confusion. Even
today some of the titles used can still be found, so that a station such
as 'Bedford Midland Road' would tell the intending traveller that this
was the Midland Railway's station, and later, after grouping, that it
was the LMS and after nationalisation British Railways London
Midland Region.

Stations, even small ones, had a substantial staff and a clear hierarchy, at the top of which was the station master. Below him there
would be ticket inspectors and porters, sometimes a porter-signalman
who doubled up and was training to become a signalman. There might
be a goods depot attached to the station with its own team. There
would also be clerks, including the booking clerks, who saw themselves as being a cut above the other railwaymen because they were
salaried, not given a weekly wage.

A Day at Thornton Abbey

Arthur Wardle was the station master at Thornton Abbey, on the
London & North Eastern Railway. His was a small station, as we will
see, mainly handling goods but with a seasonal passenger traffic.
Despite this, he seems to have been a man of ambition and some
education as he was an associate member of the Institute of Transport,
which is now the Chartered Institute of Transport & Logistics, and
would have taken examinations which would have included papers
on his particular mode of transport and one other.

> Travellers in fast trains running through small wayside stations
> have often commented on the 'outlandish situation' and seem to
> place them in a category comparable with the Toll Gate Houses
> still found upon the King's Highway.

Few people have any idea of their usefulness or activity, and out of several remarks made to me I conceived the idea of logging a day's work.

I take a normal spring day and enter my office at 8.15am to attend to passengers and open letters before the 8.38 up and 8.39 down passenger trains. These away I ascertain stock of the single twenty-wagon capacity goods siding, and find seven inwards loaded and ten empty wagons, the latter swept out ready to load.

Unloading of inwards grain and fertilizer is proceeding, and I note that only one of these three wagons is suitable to reload.

Returning to the office I find I have definite orders, so 'phone for prospects of loading and am satisfied.

The Daily Stock Report is compiled and cash remittance made up. Sort correspondence into priority order, but leave it to assist unloading of tranships from Up pick up goods on far platform: 17.1.0 [it is not clear what this means, but given the fact that a hand barrow was used, it seems to have been 17 stone 1 lb 0 oz and unlikely to be 17 cwt] of sundries which the Lad Porter and myself barrow round to warehouse. This is the smallest room on the premises, and I suggest a van for overflow.

Attend 9.57 up train with cash bag, then sort inwards invoices, and advise goods, including a van load of sugar beet seed.

Run out to 10.36 down passenger, and see the Goods Yard is now busy. I note that the day of horses is not past, for at 10.45am there are in the yard three farm wagons, four rulleys and one cart, with fourteen horses, in addition to three motor wagons bringing in or taking away goods.

Entering goods received in Warehouse book I note thirty items, which is exceptional. Report discrepancies and headings, the latter frequent, as are subsidiary to another station in postal address.

Four public inquiries in succession, and calls to effect delivery of goods to the public, as the Lad Porter is 'lamping' (refilling oil lamps) three-quarters of a mile away.

I now have orders for outward loading: labels and invoices, and arrange with Control for pick up working to enable clearance of sufficient wagons to make room for inwards goods and empties.

A knock on the wall reminds me it is 12.30pm and I am late for lunch, so lock up and go [he would have had had a house at the station, so this was probably his wife knocking. His lunch was soon interrupted].

At 12.55, wanted on Circuit – Control request to expedite Down pick up. To do so I assist transhipping and tell Guard to pick up five loads and three empties; detach his five empties and get off, leaving further shunting to future train.

Finishing lunch I am out for 1.32pm passenger and assist members of the public by whispering 'which is the best wood for primroses', and promise to look up the service and fare to 'Admiral Hinton', also which route I would recommend [clearly visitors coming for a springtime walk in the wood. The latter passenger meant Hinton Admiral on the Southern Railway's mainline from Waterloo to Bournmouth].

It is my lot now to accompany an irate farmer to inspect a new seed drill that has arrived with a bent axle, and report refusal. Whilst in the Yard, I determine the wagons to be loaded this afternoon, with an eye on the elimination of shunting time.

The weighing of smalls and invoicing of outwards traffic has thrown me late; I must hurry to catch only post dispatch at 3.30pm with advices &c. A public inquiry *re* traffic eighteen months ago calls for attention; and dispatch of time sheets and paybill is essential.

At 4.30 enter up charges on four wagons sent 'W.C. & A', and follow up by trying to trace origin of sacks that have been shuffled between merchants many miles away.

It is 5 o'clock: take off ticket rack and balance cash. Realising it is March 28 and nothing done towards month end, I decide to abstract, but rediscover Traffic Analysis and complete the extension slips in that week's work.

Passenger trains 5.30 Up and 5.34 Down, the latter followed by pick up, which takes other three loaded wagons, detaches two, and fouls the foot crossing for 6.9 Up passenger train, necessitating me taking parcels over wagons, and entertaining alighting passengers until Goods departs,

I decide 'Enough', and at 6.25 leave the Porter in charge, with instructions to call me if he is in doubt.

I should explain that the staff here consists of Porter, Lad Porter and myself.

Primarily a goods station, our activity starts at the end of July with green peas, followed by grain, sugar beet and cabbages until early April.

During last year we forwarded:

	Tons	Receipts	Wagons
Goods	1,666	£1,698	562
Minerals (Sugar Beet)	1.063	£172	103

Cabbages, mainly in piped wagons for London markets, accounted for 779 tons, earning £956 of the Goods figures.

Farm produce and a village industry bring in a fair revenue to Parcels and Miscellaneous Account, which during 1934 totalled £233.

About Easter the visitors to the Abbey ruins begin to arrive, and at Holiday week-ends we are fully occupied shepherding parties of school children.

There seems at the time to have been a tendency for people turning up at the station to buy tickets or make a reservation to ask for the stationmaster, rather than simply deal with the booking clerk, although clearly at Arthur Wardle's station he and his small team did virtually everything.

Can I see the Stationmaster?

Writing from the viewpoint of someone working at a larger station, presumably Scarborough, W.J. Midgley describes how a typical passenger makes a reservation.

'Good afternoon, can I see the stationmaster, please?' On inquiry as to the nature of the business on which the lady specially desires to see the stationmaster, she replies: 'Oh, I wanted him to reserve me a seat in the London train tomorrow afternoon.' When told that this could be arranged with the clerk to whom she had addressed her query, the lady produces a small notebook with train times she has obtained from the inquiry office, and says: 'I would like a seat reserved for me in a corner, you know, the window side, and one facing the engine, Can you reserve it in a compartment in the centre of the coach, as I do not like to travel over the wheels. Oh, by the way, I should like to be near the dining car. Are there many seats reserved in this train? Yes, please, third class, I can't afford to travel first. Do I take this ticket? Thank you very much, I am afraid I have given you a lot of trouble? Did I tell you I wanted to ride in a non-smoker? Thanks so much. Good day.'

This is one of several thousands of holidaymakers who are to be dealt with, and the patience of the 'reservation clerk' is sorely tried.

The lady obviously was concerned about her comfort and knew what she wanted, although it seems odd that she left the important point about travelling in a non-smoker to the end. The booking clerk should have offered her the choice, although most railway compartments were smokers at this time and she should have known this. Nevertheless, she was very polite and did not resort to bullying, unlike some, as Midgley continues his anecdote.

Often the retired army major type of individual calls to book accommodation, and in stentorian tones demands a seat reserving a week ahead, and threatens to write to his director friend if his wishes cannot be absolutely guaranteed.

Cases have been known where a passenger, unable to find a single seat in a train, has come to the office to book a seat in that train and expressed himself highly dissatisfied with the organisation. 'I'm a shareholder, you know, and you will hear further about it,' he says, when it is suggested that he should travel by a later train in which a seat could easily be reserved.

Baggage for the Continent

Obviously travel to and from continental Europe pre-dated the railways, but the railway age saw marked growth in such travel. The need to safeguard its premium traffic from growing competition from air transport was behind the Southern Railway's innovations including the all-first-class Pullman 'Golden Arrow' boat and later its through London to Paris overnight sleeper service, the 'Night Ferry'. Just to cover all of its options, the Southern also opened the first airport station at Shoreham (now known as Brighton Airport) and then a station at Gatwick Airport, as well as asking if it could take over the European services of Imperial Airways!

Nevertheless, these were the days before easy international travel. Passports were essential, and baggage was often opened for inspection by customs officials, and this could make a train journey through several different countries tiresome. Baggage had to be registered, and the *Southern Railway Magazine* carried an article about this, although in typical Southern fashion, it was not by an actual baggage clerk but was more in the nature of an essay by a certain R.W. Tuck, who worked at Waterloo.

> What is this registration of continental luggage that one hears about vaguely from time to time? Come with me to Victoria Station, where far more registered baggage is dealt with than at any other station in Great Britain, and we will investigate.
>
> First of all you are set down with your luggage, from your private car, taxi, or other vehicle, outside the continental departure platforms. An outside porter will quickly load your trunks, etc., on to a barrow and will precede you into a spacious luggage hall. In the centre of this hall you will see the two large dials of two weighing machines. None of your old-fashioned weights and scales normally associated with railway stations. The moving of a small lever causes a pointer to swing around the dial and rest on the correct net weight (excluding that of the barrow or trolley). You will be handed a weight docket by the machine operator, showing the number of packages to be registered and their total weight. This individual will also direct you to one side of the luggage hall, where you will see a row of ten windows. You will not see them all open unless you are there at a very busy time, such as the week before Christmas; but seven or eight of them are in use at once at certain busy times of the day.
>
> You select the most vacant of the open windows and in your turn present your weight docket to the clerk. He will enquire where you are going and ask to see your tickets. We will assume that your wife and yourself are travelling to Milan by the 2 o'clock boat train from Victoria, and that you have three pieces of luggage weighing 154-lb. If you have seat reservations on the French train they will probably be pinned in your tickets. If not, the clerk will most certainly question you on that point, for they enable him to see at a glance which way you are travelling through Switzerland. This information is not ascertainable from the ticket itself, which is alternatively routed.
>
> The through train to Milan, which you intend to catch at Boulogne, divides just before it reaches Switzerland, and although

each portion eventually reaches Milan, they traverse Switzerland by two entirely different routes. The real reason for the correct routing of your luggage is that the customers authorities at the Italian frontier may desire to examine it, and if you were not on the same train yourself they would probably hold up your luggage for some days.

Several Charges in One

Having at length ascertained the correct route for your luggage to travel, the clerk will produce a book of printed tickets and labels for Milan. You will see him write down the number of passengers and pieces of luggage, and the total weight of 154-lb. Then he will deduct 132-lb, being the free allowance through England and France of 66-lb per passenger, leaving the excess weight of 22-lb. Then he will begin to put down item after item of charges, and you will glare through the window-bars anxiously, mentally imploring him to stop and add up the bill before it gets too heavy.

You may perhaps express a desire to know the nature of all these items. If so, the clerk will inform you rapidly, '1s a package registration fee; 6s 3d for excess weight through England and France; 12s 10d Swiss and 2s 4d Italian charges on the gross weight; 3d Italian tax; 8d Boulogne tax; 2d a package French handling charges; total to pay, £1 5s 10d'. You may feel slightly staggered, but you will have to pay up and be thankful your wife is accompanying you, for with only one passenger ticket you would have to pay nearly a pound more. On the other hand, if you were alone, you would probably take much less luggage.

As soon as you have settled with the clerk at the window, he will give you the top copy of the luggage ticket which he has made out in triplicate, for you to reclaim your luggage with at Milan. He will then hand you three printed labels from London to Milan which will bear a number corresponding to that printed on your luggage ticket, and also three larger labels bearing the number of the train which goes through from Boulogne to Milan. You must see these labels affixed to your luggage, which is then out of your charge until you reach Milan, except that you must be prepared at the Italian frontier in case the custom authorities wish to examine it.

800 Different Ticket Books

Before you take your seat in the train let us glance inside this luggage office. You will see a long counter reaching the whole length of the office above which is the row of ten windows previously mentioned. Behind the clerks as they stand at the counter windows are large cases composed of hundreds of racks, each rack contains a book lying flat. There are over 800 different books of luggage tickets in daily use. They are arranged in these racks in the order of different routes, and alphabetically within each route. Inside the cover of each book the rate to be charged to that particular station is inserted.

The luggage tickets are always made out in triplicate; one is for the passenger, one is for the guard of the train, and the third is retained for audit purposes. The sets of tickets are numbered consecutively throughout each book, and to each set are attached six labels bearing similar numbers. If the number of packages comprising one consignment are less than six the unused labels are destroyed; if more than six an extra set of tickets is used.

Different Labels for Different Trains

You will observe a smaller rack filled with different labels for various continental trains, such as the 'Orient Express', 'Calais–Mediterranean Express', 'Vienna Express', etc. These are affixed to luggage when necessary in addition to the numbered labels showing the destination station. You will realise from this that the luggage clerk has to know the timings of all the chief continental expresses from the French ports, and from Paris, and why he must make so certain as to whether the passenger has seat reservations or sleeping-car tickets on any special French train.

Luggage is registered from this office for the following continental services:

 9.00am   Folkestone–Boulogne
10.00am   Dover–Ostend
11.00am   Dover–Calais ('The Golden Arrow')
11.15am   Dover–Calais
 2.00pm   Folkestone–Boulogne
 2.00pm   Dover–Ostend
 4.00pm   Dover–Calais
 6.10pm   Gravesend–Rotterdam (not Sundays)

Nearly 300,000 pieces of luggage are registered in the course of a year, whilst on some busy days 800 pieces are sometimes registered by one service. Luggage by the Newhaven–Dieppe route is registered at another office near the departure platform of that train [This would be at the 'Brighton' side of Victoria, while the luggage hall covered here is for the Eastern Section or the old London Chatham & Dover station].

By adding the number of pieces dealt with at that office we arrive at the yearly total of about 350,000 pieces of luggage registered for the continent from Victoria Station.

A large amount of routine duty is involved in connection with this work. It mainly consists of recording, in books and on monthly abstract sheets, full particulars of each registration.

The whole work is very interesting and is of a specialised nature. It certainly enables the clerks to attain an excellent knowledge of European travel, theoretically, at any rate.

At this time the stations handling continental boat trains would also have included Waterloo and Liverpool Street.

The Junior Porter

The LMS Magazine made a point of having a page called 'Our Juniors Page' for those of its employees under the age of twenty years. The range of jobs that these people could fulfil was limited, but included page boys in the hotels and junior porters and junior clerks, but there was no such thing as a junior fireman, still less a junior engine driver, on the footplate, for the simple reason that such people were spending their time working their way up from locomotive cleaners. These were days when most children left school at fourteen years of age, and the proportion of the population staying at school until they were eighteen was small, and fewer still went to university, although the number of places was growing due to the new 'red brick' universities.

Much, but not all, of this account is written in the third person, although the junior porter is identified as G. Netherwood, and one suspects that the editor had more than a hand in the effort.

What ... is the tale told by that junior ever in the public eye – the junior porter? Let us take an early turn of duty in the summer. The alarm breaks forth, and with a Spartan-like effort he springs from bed and silences its brazen-clanging. There is no time to waste and soon he is hurrying to work, admiring as he goes the glories of the sunrise … Soon the station comes in sight, and he prepares himself for the day's task. The booking office now being unlocked, his first thought is for the time book, in which he neatly inserts '6.10*am*' before commencing work. Waiting rooms must be unlocked and dusted, and the station gates also have to be opened.

Scarcely has he finished dusting than the first train arrives, forerunner of many others. Hurrying to the ticket barrier, he collects the tickets and keeps an alert eye for any carriage doors that may not be properly shut; for a swinging door and a tunnel mouth are very nasty when they meet each other! The guard gives the right away, and our junior watches the train depart, noting the dozing passengers in the comfy compartments.

The 'rush hour' approaches. Every station worker will tell you of that period, which is, of course, more in evidence at bigger stations than the smaller ones, but every station has its 'rush hour' and ours is no exception. The we see the guards standing impatiently by their brakes, fingering their whistles and itching to give the 'right away'. They cannot go, however, until they see the porter's arm jutting out at the front of the train. It is 8.39am, and the train is due away, but still the passengers come scurrying down the footbridge steps. And when the train *does* leave, we are often besieged by angry passengers who have missed it, swearing that the station clock is wrong, and that their watches, which have not lost one-fifth of a second in fifteen years, are right! Ignoring their threats of court-martial, we calm them as best we may, and politely tell them there is another train at 9.01am. So it goes on, until after various tasks, such as handling parcels and luggage, and keeping the station neat and tidy, the Junior Porter views with relief the milk train puffing up the bank, *his* last train for the day.

Occasionally, we have a break from the usual routine.

A horse is on the line, and a junior is sent to deal with it. With a swagger that would bring praise from Tom Mix [the cowboy film star], he sallies forth, and finds, perhaps, a wicked-looking dapple grey mare which had broken through the fencing, trespassing upon the Company's premises, and eyeing him with suspicion. By dint of coaxing and threatening he manages to get the obstinate quadruped back to the field where it belongs, and then he returns to the station and informs the ganger of the circumstances. Fate, with its usual love of variety, may send a cow, a sheep, or even a dog, to test our abilities as herdsman!

On the face of it, a Junior Porter's lot may seem to many very ordinary. But in point of fact it is often very interesting, and sometimes brings amusing episodes as well. So that when his twentieth birthday arrives, and he enters man's estate, the average Junior can look back with a certain amount of pleasure at his early experiences and the difficulties he faced and overcame when he first entered the service as a raw lad from school.

Of course, the amusement may have been unintentional. The same issue tells the story of a passenger on a long journey sticking his head out of the window when the train stops at a station and asking the porter whether he could get any liquid refreshment.

'No, sir,' replied the porter. 'Only tea and coffee, sir.'

The Editor as a Goods Porter

Edward Hadley's mission, while editor of the *Great Western Railway Magazine*, to gain first-hand experience of as many jobs on the railway as possible so that he could write a book on 'Accident Prevention for Railway Workers' eventually found him in the role of a goods porter at Paddington goods station. Of course, he told his readers about his experience, in the third person. This was a much shorter piece than usual and appears to have been a 'taster' for a much longer article.

On commencing he was attached to a gang comprising a checker, a caller-off, and three other porters, and his hours of duty were from 3.00pm to midnight. His work consisted mainly of trolleying 'outwards' goods from road vehicles to the trucks that were being loaded at the various platforms. It was a revelation to him to discover that a Paddington goods porter, in the course of one day's trolleying, covers at least fourteen or sixteen miles.

Remaining for a while on the 'outwards', Mr Hadley participated in the work of calling-off, checking, loading, sheeting, and roping of goods; and afterwards was transferred to the 'inwards' work, where his turn of duty commenced at 2.00am.

He says that his transformation into 'Porter No. 229' has identified him with a body of very fine fellows, whose friendliness has
been unbounded.

Last year, on British railways, there were 2,909 accidents to
goods porters, which number worked out to one accident for
every seven men. Most of the accidents consisted of contusions
of limbs, cuts and sprains. Accidents to loaders and sheeters
numbered 859, or one accident for every nine men. Checkers were
more fortunate, their accidents being equal to one for every
sixteen men.

Clearly, his planned book was much needed, if those involved would
take the time to read it. That said, the news item was accompanied by a
small photograph showing Hadley with a two wheeled trolley, on
which was one box or carton on top of which was a very much larger
crate, and he was depicted holding the trolley handle with one hand
while the other steadied the crate! Not at all safe!

Of Dogs and Booking Clerks

Booking clerks seem to have gained themselves not just more column
inches but more pages than other grades of railwaymen. Possibly this
was because they were the most literate outside the management
structure, or perhaps they had more time and a relatively comfortable
ticket office in which to work, although as we will see, they did other
things than simply sell tickets. One LMS booking clerk was actually
favoured with not just an article on his day's work, but a series which
was virtually an autobiography and entertained the reader to his
experiences when he ventured abroad, and his experiences were
coloured somewhat by the fact that he was no linguist and didn't even
seem to have a phrase book.

Clearly, some aspects of their work stuck in their memories more
than others, and for one J.H. Thompson, writing in the *LMS Magazine*,
it was the question of tickets for dog.

It will probably be a matter of surprise to the present generation of
booking clerks to hear that less than fifty years ago there was as
much formality to go through in issuing ticket for a dog with a
passenger at a fare of 3d as to book a pair of horses to the North
of Scotland at a charge of £10 or more. Formidable documents

known as Horse, Carriage and Dog Tickets were used and filled up, in duplicate; sending and receiving stations had to be inserted, passenger's name asked for, and signature obtained, this signature being necessary to limit the Company's liability in case of injury or loss of the animal during transit. Many were the complaints made by the owners, and much banter, sarcasm, and even abuse did we poor HC&D clerks have to hear on account of the long and cumbersome procedure.

One instance in particular comes to my mind. Sir Henry Campbell-Bannerman came to my window one day for a dog ticket to Stirling, and while I was making out the ticket, he said – in effect – 'When will you English companies be more up-to-date with these dog tickets? I have just paid £6 or £7 for her ladyship and myself, and then have all this fuss and ceremony to pay a few shillings for the dog.' He was very courteous and tolerant, and when I said that I was only executive and not legislative, Sir Henry said, 'Oh, I am not blaming you personally; it's the system that's at fault. It is entirely out-of-date – far behind the Continental method.'

Some time after this we received instructions that card tickets would be supplied for dogs with passengers, provided the value of each animal was not more than £2. The Chief Booking Clerk at Euston at this time was Mr Thomas Gray, and a better man for the office could not be. He was strict disciplinarian, a terror to the wrong-doer, but loyal and staunch to any of the clerks who obeyed orders issued from his private office. I was then one of the HC&D clerks, and on receipt of the circular announcing this innovation, Mr Gray had me before him and said we must inquire of all passengers asking for dog tickets if the value of the animal was over £2, and if the answer was 'Yes', the old style of paper ticket must still be obtained. When I suggested that surely the onus of declaring a higher value rested with the passenger, he said, 'No; *you* must ask, for the Company's protection,' and this being so it had to be done, for none of Mr Gray's clerks ventured to argue with him.

Shortly after, a lady came to the office for a dog ticket. 'Are you travelling with the dog, madam?' I asked. 'Yes'. 'Is its value over £2?' – and for an answer the lady walked away. A few minutes later up came a porter saying that one of the directors wished to see the Chief Booking Clerk with the clerk who had refused to issue a dog ticket to his wife. Mr Gray and I went to the gentleman accordingly, and he asked Mr Gray why his clerk was asking these unnecessary questions now that a simplified form of dog ticket had been introduced. Then said Mr Gray: 'I am very sorry if any trouble has been caused, but if anyone is to blame it is I, for I told the clerk to ask the question as to value.' The Director at once replied, 'If the clerk is carrying out your instructions, I have no more to say to him,' and I was at once released from the dreaded interview.

Now it is as easy to take a ticket for a dog as for a passenger.

It seems that this account related to London & North Western Railway days, for apart from anything else, the LMS acted quickly to remove its directors from Euston to a new office building, Euston House, created to hold the much enlarged headquarters of the grouped company. Between the wars, one of the advertising campaigns on which the 'Big Four' collaborated was one that encouraged passengers to take their dogs with them, even promising the availability of water at stations. One wonders if this is still so today.

Reminiscences

Once again we have J.H. Thompson, a booking clerk writing at some length, although on this occasion identified only by the initials 'J.H.T.' As the earlier tale indicates, he had clearly worked on the railway for many years as he joined the London & North Western in 1875 at the age of seventeen years, and was still working for its successor, the LMS, many years later. Unusually, he also gives details of his starting salary, and at the time there did not seem to be any distinction between juniors and adult employees. He had in fact done better for himself than expected as he had applied for the position of parcel porter, been examined and interviewed by the company, and given the post of booking clerk at Lichfield.

My commencing salary was similar to the stipend of Goldsmith's village pastor in *The Deserted Village*, viz £40 a year, and like him I was 'passing rich', for this was more than double my previous income. For board and lodgings I paid 13s a week, and when there were five Saturdays in the month, I paid my landlady £3 5s of the £3 6s 8d received, leaving me with 1s 8d for other expenses. This led me to decide to board myself. My lodgings were near Trent Valley Station, but the shops were a mile or more away, and to get my provisions, etc., I was glad to have the kindly offices of the driver of the one-horse 'bus which ran between the city and the station. He was John Ellis, a man of whom I think with great affection, and wonder if he is still living. He was quite a local character, very droll with his remarks, and as imperturbable as Sam Weller ... This man's so called 'bus was a covered waggonette, known by many names but the horse had only one pace. A commercial traveller, who was a regular passenger, being in rather a hurry one day, exclaimed to Ellis, 'Now, driver, can't you go a little faster?' 'Yes, sir, came the reply, '*I* can, but the horse can't.'

Like most growing lads I always felt the pull of the bed when it was time to leave it, and one morning I woke very late. Hurriedly slipping on my clothes, I ran to the station, and as I went, knew something was wrong, but dared not stop to see what it was. On entering the booking hall I saw there was but one prospective passenger and that was the Bishop, Dr Selwyn. When he came to the window to book he said very gravely, 'Young man, does not the North Western Company give its servants sufficient time to dress?' and, on turning round, I found that only one brace was in its proper place, the other was hanging down behind me, and it was that had dangled between my legs as I can!

It is not everyone who has held the IOU of a bishop, but I have. Dr Selwyn died, and was succeeded by Dr Maclagan, afterwards Archbishop of York, who once came to the station and told me he had no money with him, would I let him have a 3rd single to Euston, and he would send the fare to me. I consented, and he left me an IOU on his visiting card. Very promptly Dr Maclagan sent the remittance with a request that I would return his 'card' – he did not say 'My IOU!' That letter is now amongst my autographs.

In a cathedral city like Lichfield, one came into personal touch with many of the clergy, who then did their travelling by train, for motor cars were still in the future. Amongst them was a canon who used to give a piece of beef and a glass of elderberry wine to the station staff ever Christmas. There was an Archdeacon who borrowed 5s of me, and to whom I had to make at least one written application before he repaid it. There was also the Dean; Dr Bickersteth – who was always most suave and courteous; it was a pleasure to do anything for him ...

... For a young man to get a general and practical knowledge of railway working there is nothing like a few years at a country station. In my case the Booking Office was also Parcels Office, Lost Property Office, Cloak Room and Telegraph Office. The telegraph instruments were not in my charge, but with a desire to learn all that I could, I made myself acquainted with their working. This came in useful, for one night when staying very late to balance the monthly classification, and long after the station and its approach had been closed, I heard someone walking about, and trying the outer door. The came a rapping at the window near me, and enquiring what was wanted, a man's voice replied, 'I want to come in.' 'Well, you can't, 'I said, 'the station is all locked up,' and the welcome sound of retreating footsteps was then heard. My relief, however, was but momentary, for directly afterwards the man was in the office, having scaled a wall to get to the platform. Not liking the manner of his advent nor the appearance of his person, I telegraphed to the Signal Box in the yard, asking for the Night Foreman to come at once as I had a man in the office. He soon came, had a few words with the intruder, and put him off the premises.

The next day enquiries were made, and my unwelcome visitor turned out to be a lunatic who had escaped from the County asylum at Burntwood, some six miles from Lichfield!

Thompson was never backward in putting down his personal experiences and connections, much of which had little or nothing to do with railways and their working. Nevertheless, there are others that tell us much of an age that is long past.

Prior to the introduction of motors, when the gentry went for their holidays they not only travelled by rail themselves, but sent their horses, carriages and luggage too – a valuable source of revenue to the railway companies. Here is a typical application, made by the Bishop of Lichfield, for travelling facilities for his establishment:

Family carriage for 10 or 12 1st class passengers
8 or 10 servants
Horse box for 2 fully sized horses, 2 ponies (one very small)
Carriage truck for 1 4-wheeled carriage

When the charges were made up there was an odd half-penny in the total, and the Bishop made out the cheque, as most people would have done, for that amount short. After considering a moment, I said: 'There's another half-penny, my Lord.' Looking straight at me, he said in grave tones: 'Do you want the half-penny?' 'Well, my Lord, if you do not pay it I shall have to.' He then raised the Episcopal apron, found his pocket, produced a long beaded purse, and extracted the required bawbee!

The Junior Clerk

This is another account from the 'Our Juniors Page' of the *LMS Magazine*, and the contributor, one Tom Cooper, seems to have written this one himself, which is not too surprising as he is a clerical worker. Information on pay scales can be misleading, so it is interesting to note that this young man can afford a motorcycle, which suggests that his remuneration was good for his age, as even motorcycle ownership was out of the reach of many at the time.

I have been fortunate in being appointed to a fairly busy station in East Perthshire. My home is approximately eleven miles away and I motor cycle to and from the station daily.

My hours of duty are as follows: On my early shift I start at 7.00am and finish at 5.30pm, although some nights it is after 6 o'clock before I cease work owing to heavy game traffic coming in from the surrounding district. On such occasions I am asked why I am late and so on, but one can hardly cease work in the middle of a large consignment just because it is time for 'knocking off'. At our station, of course, the motto is, 'one good turn deserves another', so my superior officer does the same on early shift.

It takes me about twenty-five minutes to make the journey from my home to the station, so that I have to depart at 6.30am in order that there may be no hurry. There are some mornings, however, when I oversleep myself, with the result that I have to 'put in a sprint.' I don't think, however, that I have ever been guilty of being late for my work.

On my arrival at the station I receive the keys of the safe, ticket case, etc., from the stationmaster, and then write up the parcels that come off the first train on the carter's sheet. By the time this is done, passengers will probably be waiting to book for the first train out, which is at 7.25am. There is no train between this and 8.26am, so I occupy my time writing up the train book, stamp book, returns, etc., for the coming month. There are sure to be people coming in with parcels, too, so that time soon slips round to 9 o'clock, when there is usually a good number of passengers to be booked.

From 9.00 to 10.00am is my breakfast hour. After it I go over to the goods office and assist the clerk there with the invoices, etc. At noon he goes to his lunch and I am left to work until 1 o'clock, when he resumes work. I then relieve the booking clerk from 1.00 to 2.00, which is his dinner hour. When he comes back I take my dinner and then return to the goods office and work there until 5.00pm, invoicing traffic and making out labels for wagons. There is a jute factory in the town, and we do a fairly large trade with it. On my late shift, I commence at 10.00am and finish at 7.30pm.

The one shift is as good as the other, with the exception, of course, of Saturdays, when the clerk who is on the early shift gets the afternoon. This day is usually the busiest one of the week, as the goods department closes at noon, and we have almost the same amount of traffic to book in half the time. There is always a large number of passengers on Saturday, most of whom go to Dundee which is the nearest big town to us. In the afternoon I make up the time sheets and wages paybills in time for their being sent away on the Monday.

There are occasions when I find myself in a dilemma, and on such occasions I immediately go to the stationmaster and him for help, at the same time impressing his advice on my memory for future use.

Any spare time I spend practising shorthand, as I am taking lessons in preparation for my examination.

Some people seem to think that office work must be very monotonous, but I never find it so because there is always something new cropping up in the course of the day's routine. Another thing that makes life a pleasure to me here is the cheery and friendly way in which everyone goes about his work.

The Loader

Not every station was for passengers, for many simply handled goods, and were known variously as goods stations or goods depots, while just to confuse people, the LMS and GWR at least would also speak and write of freight trains. Many organisations would have described the people loading and unloading the goods wagons as 'porters', but the LNER at least described them as 'loaders'. It is interesting that one of these was tempted to, or persuaded, to write about his work for the *London & North Eastern Railway Magazine*, and if it was 'ghosted' for him, at least on this occasion the writer wrote in the first person and did not wander from third to first and back again.

The man in question was Charles E. Mair, who worked at Aberdeen Guild Street, which he describes as a depot and, as I can't find it in the passenger timetables, I can only assume that it was a goods depot without passenger facilities. Separating the two had advantages as goods depots needed good access for vehicles, while most passengers could walk, and in any case passengers did not want their way obstructed by large quantities of goods, although milk and newspaper trains usually used passenger stations. There was another advantage, since it segregated employees as passenger porters could earn gratuities and those handling goods couldn't.

This again is another glimpse of a different world, as Mair's wide variety of goods handled tells us. I also doubt today whether many would talk or write about 'dead meat', reasoning that 'meat' is never alive.

Aberdeen (Guild Street) Station must, in my opinion, be one of the more interesting depots on the system. By interesting, I mean the different varieties of goods we may be called upon to deal with during a day's work ...

First and foremost we have the dead meat traffic to London. If it is true what Napoleon said about an army marching on its stomach, then London must have a goodly number of hikers, judging by the amount of dead meat that is sent from Aberdeen to the Metropolis. Some weeks an average of between 120 to 130 tons of meat are sent away. The method of loading the dead meat consists of hanging short sides on the bars of meat vans, or the 'M' type of container, with an average of 30 sides in each. Long sides, being too lengthy to hang, are laid down on the floor of the vans, with an average of fourteen sides in each; mutton being hung to the extent of sixty to each vehicle. Aberdeenshire, being famous for its cattle breeding, it is essential that the dead meat arrives in London in as prime a condition as possible, and this is where the Railway Company plays its part. Just how's this for service? On three days a week we have a fully loaded 'perishables' train which leaves Aberdeen at 10.45am and arrives in London about 11.00pm with the meat in good time and condition for the following day's sales. A further aid to the condition of this traffic is the 'M' type of container which is now in general use. Coincident with the meat traffic we also have large quantities of hides and sheep skins to deal with.

Besides being an important agricultural centre, Aberdeen is also an important fishing port, and here London traffic again comes into the limelight, for on Saturdays alone – when the freight service is quite suitable – as many as 30 tons of fish are handled at the goods department, besides several tons for other parts of the country.

Being now 'fed up' with foodstuffs, I take a hand in the loading of one of Aberdeen's staple industries – granite. Which town in Britain and overseas has not got its quota of Aberdeen granite? Several wagons for home or export are forwarded each day. Paper making is also an important industry of this town, there being two large mills in the city – one concerned in the manufacture of envelopes and writing paper, and the other chiefly in the production of paper for leading newspapers. The former firm's traffic is divided between fully loaded containers and sundry lots for all over the country. The output from the other mill consists chiefly of reels weighing on an average 7 cwt each. To prevent chafing or rubbing against each other, these reels are specially protected by special 'beds' in the form of packed canvas. These 'beds' measure 30 feet long and 6 feet wide, and the folds lie between the reels – two abreast – the reels being tightly jammed, thus reducing the danger of damage to a minimum. As much as 70 tons of this traffic has been dealt with in one day.

Hello! What's this? A load of machinery from one of the engineering works has just arrived, and as the special wagons required are at hand I am 'told off' not to keep the load waiting. This particular lot takes the form of crane work in parts for South [sic] firms, and is dealt with at frequent intervals.

The aforementioned 'heavy' traffic employs me for the good part of a day, but contrast it with the rest of the time in the loading away of forwarded; the calling off of received sundries; and various odd jobs, and you must admit, reader, that we loaders at Aberdeen (Guild Street) besides having a busy day, have also a most interesting one.

Although there would have been small cranes and derricks to help with the heavier work, including moving the 'M' containers between railway wagon and road wagon, there would still have been relatively little mechanisation by modern standards. Fork lift trucks were unknown, and even for the passenger porters, the small tractors towing several trailers along the platforms did not appear until the late 1930s and early 1940s.

Chapter 3

The Station Hotel

All of the 'Big Four' railways had station hotels inherited from their predecessors, and although the impoverished Great Central left it to others to build hotels close to its London terminus at Marylebone, other more prosperous railways built hotels as resorts in their own right, with the finest example being that at Gleneagles built by the Caledonian Railway. Hotels grew up around railway stations and especially the great London termini just as they do around airports today. There was one difference, however, for many airport hotels benefit from serious flight delays when some airlines still, especially for their premium passengers, will book passengers into a hotel, but the railways never did this. Rather, the hotel was close to the railway station so that the weary traveller arriving in a strange town or city did not have far to look for accommodation.

To those railwaymen, the vast majority, working in the sheds or the workshops, or on the line, or in the signalbox or on the footplate, this side of the business was a mystery. Certainly the operational railwaymen, even with a so-called 'lodging turn' that involved an overnight stay away from home did not, unlike airline flight crew, stay in a hotel but instead a boarding house or, if there were enough of them and demand was constant, even in a hostel run by the railway. Much of what we know about these people comes from the railway magazines who felt the need to highlight the work of their wide variety of employees.

What the Head Waiter Does

The LMS Magazine was well to the fore in detailing the various occupations that its employees filled. One of these was a head waiter called W.S. Clancy, although his location was not given.

It may sound strange, but whenever I hear it said that the 'Head Waiter is that chap who wanders round, doing nothing in particular,' I regard it as a compliment. Broadly speaking, it means that our arrangements are working out so well that everything seems to happen as a matter of course, and the difficulties we are faced with are so successfully camouflaged as to seem non-existent. Nevertheless a Head Waiter's position is not so easy as it appears. Besides being responsible for the actual serving of the meals he has to see to it that members of his staff are smart in their appearance when on duty and efficient in the way they do their job. Of course, in these enlightened days, most men take the pride they should in their personal appearance, although I am afraid that there are exceptions even now, but the term 'efficient' covers a great deal, and there are those amongst us whose 'efficiency' depends upon their state of mind. I mean by this that while most men in our line of business can do well when all works smoothly, it is not so easy when there is a rush, or if a customer is at all eccentric, to keep one's equilibrium and handle cases with diplomacy; and it is just here that the Head Waiter is called in. Whether the customer's complaint is justified or not is then beyond the point; it is left to the Head Waiter to use his tact in a difficult situation.

The Need for Attention
Another responsibility of the Head Waiter's is the charge of equipment of the restaurant, which may easily be valued at hundreds of pounds sterling. This wants constant attention, not only as regards cleaning – a not inconsiderable item – but also to see that it is not lost or mislaid. A customer will, for instance, give a baby a spoon to keep it quiet, and then, quite unintentionally, of course, forget to leave the spoon behind, in the hurry and excitement of catching the train. Or, again, the smaller items are liable to get thrown away with tea leaves and other waste.

A Head Waiter's first duty is to see that all of his tables are properly laid up, and that all the silver thereon is clean and in its proper place. Then he consults the chef as to the day's menu, and when the meal commences he has the delicate job of seeing without undue ostentation, that all his customers are comfortably seated and that there are waiters in attendance on them. When many people arrive at the same time, as frequently happens at a large station, this is often rather difficult, because most are in a hurry, and all want to get away as quickly as possible.

A point of great value to a Head Waiter is the ability to remember faces, and not only this, but he ought to recollect as well the particular likes and dislikes of regular customers. People have all sorts of fads and fancies. For instance, a dish that suits the taste of one may be anathema to another, or a waiter who is welcome at one table may be disliked by certain other customers, possibly on account of some quite accidental error on his part on a former occasion.

The position of the table, too, has to be taken into account; there are people who always like to sit in the same place in the restaurant, and to keep the chosen seat vacant at the psychological moment and yet avoid offence to some customer who wants to occupy it, needs tact indeed.

The Need for Tact
Sometimes a patron will arrive cross and irritable. Something has happened during the day to upset his temper, and he comes into the restaurant annoyed with everything and everybody. Here is a problem for the Head Waiter. Courteous treatment and a nice meal well served will send the man away with a completely different outlook upon life, and a contented customer will remember us and come again; but if anything, however small, happens to incur his displeasure, it may mean trouble for the staff and loss of future business. A capable Head Waiter will go out of his way in such a case to think of little things likely to appeal to the appetite of his customer, and try to nurse him back to reasonableness by tact, attention and good food.

Besides the business man and railway traveller, there is another class of customer with which a station restaurant has to deal. I refer to such folk as naval ratings, soldiers and transmigrants who arrive *en masse* and at a moment's notice want a simple meal. To meet this sort of business and do what is required properly, quickly and smoothly requires considerable organisation, but it all comes in the day's work, and a Head Waiter who cannot handle such traffic has not completed his education.

Such are the problems Head Waiters come across, and although I have only touched lightly upon them I think I have said enough to prove that the 'chap who wanders around, doing nothing in particular' is after all earning a revenue for the Company, as well as bread and butter for himself.

What a Page Boy Does

The LMS was the single largest operator of hotels in Europe, with no less than thirty-one in Great Britain and Ireland. In addition, the company operated more than a hundred refreshment rooms as well as its dining cars on the trains. This was an important part of the business. The hotel and catering aspect of the company also had its structure, and while the head waiter was near the top of his profession, the page boy was near the bottom, hoping one day to become a waiter or a dining car steward. One who was encouraged to write about his work was young Clarence Pretty.

Like most other boys who start in our department, I wanted to get straight onto the dining cars, and I got the usual reply, namely that there was nothing doing, but I could be a page in one of the restaurants if I liked. I took the offer, and later on I was started at our biggest London terminus, where there are three busy refreshment rooms beside the restaurant and smoke-room, or 'smoker' as we call it.

My jobs at first were very simple. There were four of us lads in the room, and we had to do the sweeping up, look after the fires in winter, collect cups, plates and glasses left on the tables, &c., and make ourselves generally useful.

I hadn't been very long at this when the head waiter picked me out to fill a vacancy in the dining-room. Here everything was new to me, and it was a bit muddling at first, but I soon learned how to lay the tables properly for the various meals. There are many different kinds of knife and fork and spoon. You have to know which are the right sorts to use, and how to arrange them. It isn't as simple as it is at home – a knife, two forks and a spoon, and done with! No, you've got soup, fish, entree, joint, sweets and cheese, and each course has its own special kind of cutlery, &c., to be laid out in the proper way. Breakfast, of course, is quite different, but there are still many points to watch; for instance, you don't put the mustard on the table at breakfast like you do at other meals.

Besides laying up the tables, I have to help the waiters by acting as what we call a 'Commis', which means fetching various dishes and drinks for them to serve to visitors. This is good training. You can learn a lot about waiting if you are smart, and it will help you to become a 'chef', or full-fledged waiter, later on.

Then came another chance to gain experience. The page in charge of the 'smoker' was promoted waiter, and I was called upon to take his place. That means that between certain hours I am in charge of the smoke-room. I have to get drinks or coffee for customers there, and I hold the keys of the case where cigars and cigarettes are kept. It is a glass-fronted cabinet. We arrange the cigarette packets and cigar boxes like they do in a shop window, and I am responsible for issuing smokes and have to account for them in my cash at the end of the day.

In the 'smoker', we have quite a different class of business from that in the restaurant. Here besides coffee and the more usual kinds of liquid refreshments, all sorts of 'appetisers', many of them with queer names, are asked for. They puzzled me a lot at first, and sometimes I wondered whether customers were having a joke with the 'new boy', but I never let on that I didn't know what they meant. I just passed the order across the bar, and the young lady there has always been able to turn out what is wanted. At least, I suppose so, because I've had no complaints so far!

One is left wondering a little about the standard of staff training!

Chapter 4

The Guard

The guard was a very important member of the crew of every train, no matter how humble and regardless of whether it carried passengers or freight, or even a works department train. He had to keep a look out in case the driver missed a signal, as well as looking after passengers and any mail or parcels, or even heavy luggage, in his guard's van. On a freight train or a works train, the guard's van would be a separate wagon, but most passenger trains had a large compartment at one end of a carriage as the guard's 'van'. Unless the train was very short, it was usual for there to be a guard's compartment at each end of a passenger train as the guard had to be in the rearmost carriage in case couplings broke, when he would bring the carriage or carriages to a stand and then walk back, notifying any signal box he passed, and laying detonators on the track to warn following trains to stop. Putting one at each end spared the time and expense of shunting rolling stock at the end of the journey.

One duty that started to disappear between the wars was the use of the 'slip' carriage which needed to have a guard of its own in addition to that for the train, and this individual had to have the skill to know when to detach the slip carriage and then bring it to a halt at the platform of the station for which it was intended. This was a great convenience for passengers travelling to stations at which an express did not call, but it was a one way system as there was no reciprocal arrangement for the return journey, and the slip carriages had to be collected and returned to the main station, normally one of the London termini, from which their original express had departed. This was expensive and one reason for their gradual withdrawal.

The Guard's Day

This comes from the *LMS Magazine*, and was written by a passenger guard called James Ferguson, whose location is not given but is clearly somewhere in Scotland.

The first thing I do after I have arrived at the station to take duty for the day is to go to the guards' room and sign my name in the attendance book opposite the train which I have to work, after which I carefully scan the notice board to ascertain if any fresh instructions for the guards have been posted up during my absence. Then I unlock my press [cupboard] and take therefrom my flags, hand lamp, and kit, and proceed to my train, reaching it twenty minutes before it is due to start. I next place my equipment – not forgetting my food basket – in the van, go round the non-working side of the train to see that the doors of the carriages are all closed, the carriages properly coupled together, the brake and steam heating pipes connected and the cocks open, and the passenger communication chain indicator disc at the end of each carriage is in the right position. Then I examine the inside of each van and brake carriage on the train, see that the handbrakes are fully off and are in good working order, and that the seals on the ambulance and tool boxes are intact.

Should there be any loaded horseboxes on the train, I examine each horsebox to assure myself that the horses have been loaded in accordance with the regulations, that the doors of the horseboxes have been securely closed, and that the horses are behaving themselves as sensible horses ought, and not making frantic efforts to place their forefeet in the manger or attempting to cast themselves in the stalls, as nervous horses will sometime do when travelling by rail.

I next enter in my handbook the number, class, weight, and destination of each vehicle on the train, also see that the destination boards have been fixed on the side of each carriage, and last, but not least, that the lamp man has placed a tail lamp on the rear of the last vehicle of the train.

Let me now describe a typical trip, such as is experienced daily by guards all over the system. By the time the routine preliminaries are completed, we find the parcels porter has arrived at the door of the van with two barrow-loads of parcels traffic, a miscellaneous assortment, including newspapers, boxes of fish, two insured parcels, a dog on a chain, a box of live rabbits, and a huge bundle of letters from the superintendent's office to the staff at the various stations on the journey. The loading of all the parcels having been completed, the postman next makes his appearance with a barrow-load of mails. The loading of these is an important duty: each bag must be carefully scrutinised by the guard as the postman hands it into the van to him, then placed in station order. Should a mailbag be over-carried or put out short of the proper station, the mistake is reported to the superintendent, who writes to the guard about it.

The passengers now begin to arrive. A man comes along the platform with a bicycle and lifts it into the van, at the same time telling me he is going to A—— station. The bicycle has an excess label affixed to it, but no other label of any kind. I politely inform him that he must have an address label with his name and destination written upon it and attached to the bicycle before it can be conveyed by train. His countenance falls when he hears this. 'But I'm going with it,' he protests. To argue the point with the owner of the bicycle would only aggravate him, and perhaps lose a customer, which every railwayman must do his utmost to avoid; so I take a slip of paper from my handbook, write the man's name and destination on it, and attach it to the bicycle.

'That will do now; see that you have your bicycle labelled next time you travel by train,' I advise him.

The man thanks me, well pleased, and promises to have his bicycle properly labelled in future. The engine has now backed onto the train, and as it is within a few minutes of starting time, I hurry forward to get the number of the engine, names of the driver, and also to give the driver the weight of the train. On returning to my van, I find a porter waiting for me with a barrow-load of commercial luggage, which he and I hastily stow into it. I then test the automatic brake. After I have done so, an elderly lady accompanied by a boy and girl comes to me. 'Guard,' says the lady, 'this little boy and girl are going home to Glasgow by your train. Their mother will meet them when they arrive in Glasgow, and if you will kindly take charge of their tickets and a give a look to them on the journey I shall be greatly obliged.'

I assure the lady that I will take the children safely to Glasgow, and seat them in the compartment next to my van. 'Can I get a look at the engine, Grandma?' the little boy asks.

'Not now, Willie; you will see the engine after you arrive in Glasgow,' his Grandma replies. But time is up, and I am just going to give the driver the signal to start when I notice a woman on the platform near the front of the train holding the door of a compartment wide open and gossiping with a friend in the train.

I blow my whistle as a warning to the woman that the train is going to start, expecting that she will close the door; but she pays no attention to the warning, and continues talking, until an alert ticket examiner catches the door out of her hand and closes it, and the train starts. Incidents like this occasionally happen and are apt to try one's temper.

The first thing that I do after the train has steamed out of the station is to tackle the bundle of letters and sort them into the pigeon-holes in station order. At the first stopping station I take in twelve 10-gallon cans of milk and two live calves in sacks. The young porter soils his uniform rather badly when lifting the calves into the van, and utters a few choice remarks under his breath about calves in dirty sacks by way of relieving his feelings. The calves evidently have decided objections to being trussed up tightly in sacks, and every now and then make abortive attempts to get upon their feet, only to tumble over again.

The next station is a market town, where I unload the calves, the box of rabbits, and the dog, which has evidently had enough of railway travelling, for he bounds eagerly out of the van onto the platform. The train is delayed a couple of minutes over booked time at this station searching for an umbrella which an absent-minded passenger forgot to take along with him when he left the train at the previous station. After the train has started I hear knocking on the door of the corridor leading into my van, and upon opening it I am informed by a stout elderly gentleman, who is evidently a little short-sighted, that he cannot find his compartment, meaning the compartment he had been seated in before he went to the dining car.

I find the 'lost compartment' with very little trouble, and when returning along the corridor to the van, I look in upon the little boy and girl who are thoroughly enjoying their trip, and the boy – a bright little fellow – wants to know if our engine is a 'Royal Scot'.

But the train is now nearing the end of its journey, so I hasten into my van to make out the train journal, which must be carefully written. Amongst other particulars, the composition of the train must be shown, the number of engine and name of driver; ant time lost on journey, from whatever cause, has to be fully explained, for the punctual running of a train to schedule time is of the first importance; the pressure registered on brake gauge after the brake has been tested and throughout the journey, and if the train is steam-heated, the pressure of steam registered at certain points on the journey must also be shown; the arrival and departure times from each station – in short, the journal must be a complete record of the running of the train from the time it leaves the starting station until it arrives at the end of its journey. Any omissions or discrepancies are sure to be detected by those lynx-eyed gentlemen who check the train journals, and who will quickly call the guard to account.

Clearly, a busy and demanding role, as well as one that required tact and also the need to devote some time to the needs of passengers, including those with four legs.

The Tale of the Tail Lamp

This is also from the *LMS Magazine*, with the by-line 'Told by Itself', so doubtless ghost-written.

When you look at a train and see the magnificent engine and beautiful coaches or the heavily laden wagons, how often do you think of me, the humble little tail lamp, placed on the rear of the last vehicle? Yet, my duties are very important. Although my colour is red, I have the unique distinction of being an 'all right' signal to signalmen, telling them as I do that all my train has arrived; and if they cannot see me they stop not only my train, but hold up or delay all other trains near them until they learn all is well; whilst at night my onerous duties are increased as I have to protect my train and announce its presence to the driver of any train approaching me from the rear.

I have many friends, who know that I, like they, can only carry out my important railway duties efficiently if I am fed and kept clean and well, and I thank them for their kindness to me. Perhaps they have heard the old cannon on Dover Cliffs say: 'Use me well and keep me clean, and I'll carry a ball to Calais Green;' but I want all railwaymen, more particularly those who are specially detailed to look after me, to be my friends and to think how important I am to their welfare.

I am sure, dear Mr Lampman, you do not wish to be the cause of stopping and delaying trains, bringing disappointment to stationmasters, porters, signalmen, shunters, drivers, firemen and guards who have done their best to keep the trains on time; nor to make a guard get out of his van on a wet and stormy night just to see what has gone wrong with me; whilst I know you would be filled with remorse if you thought any of your colleagues had been hurt because I had been unable to tell a driver where my train was standing; yet all these things may happen if you do not look after me well.

Do I hear you ask how you can keep me in first-class order to avoid all these things? Well, I will tell you.

Do not send me out to work unless my case is clean and my brasses polished, so that I may be seen quite easily in the daytime; and realising my most onerous duties have to be carried out during the hours of darkness, when I must give a good, steady light, see that my lens is a clear ruby in colour and not dull. My cistern must be kept clean by washing it occasionally, and filled with petroleum or longlight oil only. No other oil will do. Be satisfied that my wick is clean and sufficiently long for the journey on which you are sending me, and remember that my light, like yourself, must have clean air, but does not like draughts, so keep my chimney clear of soot and see that my door is closed firmly shut. Finally, see that my burner is clean and fits firmly; this is most important as, if the burner jumps the least bit, out goes my light. A loose burner can be made to fit firmly by pressing it slightly at the bottom. Now I am ready to do my duty; but see that I am placed gently on to the bottom of the tail bracket, and not banged down or placed halfway down the bracket, otherwise my light my be jolted out and my train stopped as soon as it leaves the station. In return for the care you have shown me I will take my train to its journey's end without causing delay or mishap, whether it be a freight, a mere local, or the 'Royal Scot'; when the journey is over, may I ask the guard lamp man or porter, who takes me off the bracket, not to put me down in any old place where I may get broken or wet, but take me to the lamp room where I can be cleaned and well trimmed again in readiness once more to do my bit to make the LMS the Best Way.

Clearly written with safety in mind.

The Guard to the Rescue

James Ferguson was writing about a normal day's work, but there was nothing routine about the actions of Guard Watts on the Southern Railway on 18 November 1930, as described in the *Southern Railway Magazine* the following January.

> The thrilling incident which was enacted in the 8.45am train from Portsmouth to Plymouth on November 18th, when the guard came to the assistance to two warders who were endeavouring to prevent the escape of the four convicts in their charge, had a sequel at the Cannon Street Hotel on December 5th, when Mr E.C. Cox, Traffic Manager, presented Guard A. Watts, of Eastleigh, with a cheque for his 'outstanding act of courage'.

The presentation was made in the presence of several officials of the Traffic Department, in addition to inspectors and guards from all parts of the system. The Traffic Manager briefly recounted the circumstances of the case:

> Four convicts were being escorted by two warders from Winchester Prison to Princetown. As the train was running between Chandlers Ford and Romsey, one of the convicts requested to be allowed to use the lavatory. The four men, chained together, were therefore taken along the corridor by the two warders, when one of the convicts released himself and with the aid of the other prisoners commenced a desperate struggle to escape.
>
> The attention of Guard Watts was attracted by the noise and he immediately joined in the struggle with such effect there was no doubt his vigorous action prevented matters culminating more seriously than they did.
>
> The prisoner who released himself jumped from the train on to the line, receiving fatal injuries which have since formed the subject of a coroner's inquest, when Guard Watts was commended for the assistance he rendered to the warders.

Cox concluded by congratulating Guard Watts for his action and then presented him with a cheque, amounted not mentioned, as a mark of the company's appreciation of his achievement.

Chapter 5

The Wheel Tapper

The wheel tapper's proper title was the much grander, and more accurate one, of train examiner, at least on the LMS as the LNER preferred the much long title of wagon and carriage examiner. Regardless of job title, here we not only read about his work but also that of his colleague, the wagon axle oiler. Trains required much more attention during the steam era, at least while on the line, even though rolling stock was less sophisticated than today. Sealed bearings only became available towards the end of the period, and sustained high speed running meant that axle boxes became hot. Lubricants were far more primitive than those available today.

While work was generally much filthier, the lack of retention toilets meant that working on the track could be unpleasant, especially in hot weather, and not all of this material hit the track, much of it also struck the underside and axles of rolling stock.

The *London & North Eastern Railway Magazine* carried a news item about the day's work of the carriage and wagon examiner based on a short paper presented by one R. Rowe of Newcastle to the York Railway Lecture and Debating Society.

This did introduce some humour to the topic, noting that the most obvious part of the role being that of wheel-tapping and that this seemed to amuse the public. There were also jokes about the wheel tappers, including one about a wheel tapper being asked why he had to tap wheels replying: 'Blowed if I know!' Another joke apparently was about the wheel tapper who had an assistant to do the listening.

Both the pieces that follow come from the *LMS Magazine*.

The Wheel Tapper

Just to drive the point home, this piece was by-lined 'By a Train Examiner'. It is one of the most interesting descriptions of someone's role as it also throws light on much of the steam railway's rolling stock.

I suppose few people, with the exception of railwaymen, know what a 'wheel tapper' really is, and probably still fewer would recognise him under his official title of train examiner ... Before a man is promoted train examiner, he has to pass the doctor; and then there is a stiff efficiency examination to be faced, which is conducted by one of the railway company's inspectors, and requires a comprehensive knowledge of the construction and maintenance of carriage and wagon stock. If the candidate succeeds both in satisfying the doctor and in answering the inspector's questions, he will pass out as a relief man, and in due course become a qualified train examiner.

The train examiner has many responsibilities. He is responsible for the soundness of every vehicle that he examines, and should there be anything wrong with the train it is his duty to take such steps as may be necessary for its safety, even though delay and annoyance may result.

During the course of his day's work he examines at least one side of numerous trains, each of which may consist from 4 to 15 carriages, or from 30 to 100 wagons. It is his duty to satisfy himself that all working parts, such as wheels, axleboxes, springs, buffing and drawgear, brakes and inside fittings are in good order, and he must see that the tyres [not the rubber variety, but the steel tyres wrapped around the outer rim of the actual wheel. A split tyre would derail a train. Some modern rolling stock has this form of wheel construction, but most have single piece wheels] are in good condition and tight not only by tapping them with the hammer, but by carefully looking all round them. [One thing he would be looking for is a 'flat', that is a tyre partly flattened by wheels locking during hard braking, and more prone that most to splitting.] To accomplish this he must be accustomed to the different sounds made by good wheels when tapped, as there are various satisfactory 'rings', and if in any doubt must adopt one of several other ways of finding out, all of which he needs to know.

He must also give attention to the passenger communication and steam heating apparatus. Whenever a train examiner finds anything wrong, he has to determine whether or not the defective vehicle is safe to travel. If the defect is serious, he affixes a red card on each side being the words 'Not to Go', and writes on it particulars of the defects, and date. Any unauthorised person removing or obscuring train examiners' cards renders himself liable to criminal prosecution.

When a vehicle requires repairs which will not render it unfit to travel, he does not detain it but labels it at each side with green cards bearing the words 'For Repairs', and writes on them particulars of the defects. A wagon bearing these green cards may go forward with its load, but must not be reloaded until it has been repaired.

If a defective brake is found on a vehicle, it is labelled with special cards marked 'Defective Brake', and the examiner secures the brake levers so that they cannot be used. All examiners' cards give particulars of forwarding point, destination, number of vehicle, owner [Apart from rolling stock from other railways, which could even at this time be European, having crossed the Channel or North Sea on a train ferry, many wagons, especially those for coal and oil, were private owners' wagons.], date, defects, and the examiner's signature.

Whenever a vehicle has been stopped by the train examiner, he at once informs the person in charge of operations how that vehicle is to be dealt with. As soon as he has completed his examination of the train and is satisfied that all vehicles on it are in good order, he gives the 'All Right' signal by waving his hammer during the day time, or his powerful acetylene lamp at night. There are three turns of eight hours each at most examining points.

A report sheet is sent to the district carriage and wagon department foreman daily. This contains details of all vehicles the examiner has stopped, giving the same information he has entered on the cards, followed by the type of vehicle, particulars of the 'repair plates' indicating the repairing company to be advised in the case of wagons owned by private or colliery companies, etc. Particulars of the train which brings the vehicles are shown, including the booked time, engine numbers, classification of train, and any delay caused by detaching the vehicle. After this he describes defects in detail, giving information as to what in his opinion caused them.

No privately-owned vehicle is allowed on the Company's main line unless it has a registration plate at each side. These registration plates indicate that the wagon has been passed by the railway company, and is up to standard specifications and measurements. They bear the name of the registering company, registered number, and year registered, also the number of tons the wagon is allowed to carry.

In the case of a hot axlebox, he gives date and place of lifting and oiling, builder's and axlebox maker's names, and all marks on the axlebox, how lubricated, condition of lubricant, marks and conditions of bearings, and condition of the journal (which is the end portion of the axle that fits in to the axlebox, and on which the bearing sits).

A train examiner must always be on the alert to meet trains, and quick to take all the information available regarding any vehicle he has dealt with, as every train, having a booked time at all places en route, must not be held up unnecessarily. Some of the most difficult cases he has to deal with are derailments, vehicles on fire, and trains becoming divided. Passenger and fitted freight trains are those which it is most important should not be delayed.

A 'fitted freight train' is one that is fitted with automatic brakes similar to those on passenger trains. The automatic brake is a continuous brake from the engine to the guard's van, which applies brake blocks to all braked vehicles throughout the train. It is automatic because should the train become divided at any part, both portions of it would be brought to a stand by the brakes becoming automatically applied.

There are two types of brake in general use on the railways, one being the Westinghouse and the other the vacuum. In the Westinghouse the brake blocks are applied by admitting air by suitable valves at a pressure of about 70-lb per square inch on to the top of a piston. In the case of the vacuum brake, the same result is obtained by creating a vacuum each side of a piston and then by suitable valves allowing air to enter on to the bottom side of it, when the piston will rise.

In both cases these pistons are connected by suitable levers to the brake blocks, and these blocks are put 'on' or 'off' depending whether the air pressure or the vacuum is on the top of the Westinghouse piston for the vacuum piston respectively.

In the case of the vacuum brake the blocks are released by the driver creating a vacuum on both sides of the piston, when it will fall and push the brake blocks on the wheels.

In the case of the Westinghouse, the blocks are released when the piston is cut off from the air pressure in the train pipe, reservoirs, etc.

Train examiners are responsible for seeing the automatic brake is in good working order on every fitted vehicle. The coaches are periodically tested, and if the brake is in good order this is indicated by the examiner marking up the date and station at which tested, on each side of the vehicle. If on the other hand it fails the test, it is labelled to the nearest repairing shop for the necessary attention.

Train examiners must also possess a knowledge of train lighting equipment, both gas and electric. Vehicles are charged with gas from high pressure mains at each important station by means of a strong flexible pipe connecting the main with the recipient valve on the vehicle. The gas is stored in large cylinders fitted underneath the vehicle, and passes through a device known as a regulator which reduces it to low pressure before delivery to the various burners.

Electric light is provided by a dynamo which is suspended from the underframe beneath the vehicle. This is driven by a pulley fitted to the axle of the carriage wheel through a belt, the electricity generated being controlled by suitable regulators, etc., that ensure the current being delivered to the lamps at correct voltage.

Lastly, there is the duty of seeing that a sufficient supply of oil, grease, etc., is on hand for use, and that these materials are not wasted; and that vehicles which have been detained are repaired with suitable material, and are completely up to standard before they are again put into traffic.

Reading this, one wonders just how train examiners managed to do their job without delaying a train for several hours. One point he didn't make, however, was that he often didn't work on his own, but with the assistance of a wagon axle oiler, as we will see below.

A Wagon Oiler's Duties

This piece is supposed to have been written by a young man called T.J. Downing, who was based at Nuneaton. His contribution appeared on the 'Juniors Page'.

The first thing I do after I sign on at 8.00am is to walk round the platforms and goods warehouse to ascertain whether there is any material arrived for us for repairs or oiling.

Some people get the idea into their heads that we do nothing else but oil, day in and day out, but this is not the case, for in between trains we are either carting material or assisting the examiners with repairs; much depends on whether we have any loaded wagons to attend to.

My first train is the 11.10am to Liverpool, which consists mostly of fitted meat vans and loaded wagons. After that there are the repairs to see to, and of these there is a great variety, because axleboxes, buffer rods, buffer castings, buffer springs, drawbars, etc. – in fact, anything in the iron or steel line – very often want attention. Any wagon the woodwork of which is found to be damaged is labelled into the shops by the examiners.

Then come the 4.15pm to Willesden and 7.20pm 'Watfords' to oil. Each of these very often consists of over sixty wagons, sometimes goods, sometimes coal; and as there are four axleboxes on every wagon, even those of you who are not good at arithmetic will realise it is no small job to get round them all.

Now a word about the oiling of these vehicles according to rules. All common-user wagons [wagons owned by the railways] have to be oiled every three months ranging from the date the last oiler inscribed on the solebar [the exposed part of the under-frame.]. Automatic vacuum-fitted vans, brake vans, and all wagons with a carrying capacity of 15 tons and over, require attention once a month.

I carry two buckets with me, one of which is divided into two portions, holding oil and soiled waste respectively, while the other contains oiling utensils – oil syringe, waste pacer for packing waste into boxes, one spanner, and a siphon for removing water from the wells of the boxes.

There are many different kinds of axlebox, but only two kinds of lubrication, 'waste' and 'pads'. In the former type, waste is is packed into the axle box tight up to the journal; in the latter, the pad is kept in position by a spring.

When the waste is dirty or has water in it, it has to be replaced with new, which has previously been soaked. The pads are occasionally taken out and ruffed up so as to allow better lubrication, because this makes them more spongy.

The covers of many axleboxes are fitted in position with bolts, which sometimes become corroded and consequently take a deal of unscrewing. Other boxes have a simple lift up observation front, which, of course, makes them far easier to deal with.

Every now and then we have a wagon stopped for loading up scrap iron, which is rather a ticklish job. This scrap varies very much in size and weight, and I think anyone without our experience would find the wagon springs we have to handle very difficult to deal with. They say, however, once you have the 'knack', the job becomes simplicity itself, and certainly lifting springs no longer worries me as it used to. It's just a matter of practice.

Being out in all weathers, and keeping regular hours, soon made me grow, and there is no junior at Nuneaton healthier or stronger than I am.

Chapter 6

The Dining and Kitchen Cars

During the second half of the nineteenth century, catering made its appearance on the main express trains, replacing the much-detested 'refreshment stop' at places like Swindon and Preston, where passengers had to scramble out of the comfort of their railway carriage and have as little as twenty minutes to have something to eat and drink, and of course attend to other body functions. The refreshment stop not only delayed the train, lengthening the journey, it was expensive and the fare on offer was often poor. First, the Midland Railway introduced Pullman cars in 1874, and then in 1879 the Great Northern Railway introduced the first dining cars.

Although both first and third-class dining cars were provided, between the wars the introduction of buffet cars greatly enlarged the numbers able to afford to buy meals whilst travelling.

Both the LMS and the LNER carried stories about the work of the staff in their dining cars. The LNER version comes from the man himself, while that from the LMS is an interview. All four of the main line railways provided restaurant cars on their trains, while the Southern Railway and the London & North Eastern were both also providers of Pullman services. Service differed greatly from that of today, when much food preparation is conducted off the train and meals are more akin to those provided by airlines. In the days of steam, all food, other than bread, cakes and biscuits, was cooked from fresh aboard the train, including roasts. Even before this, breakfast on British Railways would see stewards walking down the aisle with a large tray from which the component parts of a British breakfast would be served as the passenger dictated.

The Restaurant Car Attendant

The *London & North Eastern Railway Magazine* carried this piece about a the day's work of a restaurant car attendant, one C.A. Scarbro; a name that sounds like an abbreviation for a seaside resort.

Twenty-three years on the Leeds and London restaurant car service, involving approximately 400 miles of travel every week-day, will serve as a modest introduction to my story of the daily round. I reside in Leeds, and my duties begin at 7.00am in preparation for the departure of the 7.50 restaurant car train, Leeds to King's Cross. Breakfast being the main meal to be served on this train, covers are laid for the normal number of diners, each person requiring fourteen pieces of silver and five pieces of crockery. The cooks are now busy at the grill studying the menu bill scheduled for the morning, whilst in another direction dry stores such as toast, rolls, patted butter, marmalade, honey and cream, are put up and allocated to the required number of tables. The preliminaries over, orders are collected and recorded against each table, and the particular viands prepared and served along with coffee and tea as quickly as possible. After the last course has been served, customers are handed dockets showing the amount due, the money is collected and eventually accounted for by the conductor at the end of the day. Before leaving the breakfast service it might be mentioned that six varieties of jams are on call, and eggs are cooked in six different ways to meet particular fancies. Light refreshments are also served throughout each journey.

After leaving Grantham the tables are cleared, all crockery washed, silver cleaned, and such utensils packed away in drawers and cupboards provided for the purpose.

Upon arrival at King's Cross, fresh supplies of food, drinks, stores and linen are taken aboard, in readiness for the luncheons and teas to be served on the return journey, the 1.30pm ex-King's Cross. Much the same process is followed here as with the first meal, except that the dishes vary and more crockery is brought into use. Teas follow the luncheons and continue to the end of the journey at 5.14pm. When the washing up and cleaning have been completed the day's work is done, and six of us retire to our homesteads. Altogether our party has put in 164 years in the profession sometimes labelled as a form of 'movies'.

Although politeness and an eagerness to please are practised to extreme limits, we occasionally stand condemned for not correctly reading the minds of our clients in addition to obeying their commands. Disputes over what has been supplied are rare, but not infrequently money has to be advanced to forgetful individuals to pay the bills, and in such cases a liberal award is usually forthcoming. During the course of my career I have awaited upon three prime ministers and many dignitaries of this country and of foreign lands.

One brief anecdote in conclusion. We very rarely cause damage or annoyance to our clients, although on the move all the time. I remember dropping a pot of hot tea over the leg of one of the passengers, and, of course, made good of a delicate situation as soon as possible. Later I was informed that my choice of a limb was seemingly at fault, for its companion was artificial. Sheer bad luck!

A choice of eggs cooked in six different ways is something that BR did not provide, even in first class.

The Dining Car Conductor

Rather than a head waiter, railway dining cars had a dining car conductor, and this is an interview with 'Head Dining Car Conductor Kent' written by 'E.D.' of the *LMS Magazine*. Its value also lies in the fact that he clearly started his service with the London & North Western Railway. He also experienced the system whereby catering vehicles were shunted to join the train rather than being part of a pre-set formation, as is the case today.

Of course, things are a bit different now. Lads are often taken direct into this department – no, not always, but in the days I'm speaking off, boys used first to serve a term as page in the refreshment rooms, and most promising amongst them were chosen to fill vacancies on the cars as they occurred.

That was how I started. I began as a page at Euston, and then became what we call a 'commis' waiter, which means, you know, a kind of assistant in the dining rooms. We had to fetch things for the regular waiters and help them generally.

I shall never forget my first trip on a dining car. It happened when I was only 15. One of the regular boys on the old 5.30pm down, which used to serve Liverpool and Manchester, was off sick or something, and I was sent to take his place.

Now the attendant in charge ... was not the best disposed of men, and I don't think he felt too kindly towards his boys. There were two of them on the train, and I daresay they caused him a bit of a worry sometimes. Anyway, this is how he greeted me the evening I first reported to him for duty. 'Oh,' he said, freezing me with a glance, 'so you've come in place of young so-and-so have you? Well, it's a bad day for you, and a worse one for me!'

No, it certainly wasn't very encouraging; but I had made up my mind to get on, and as it turned out, he wasn't such a bad sort after all, so long as you did your work properly. When we got to Manchester that night he took me to his 'digs' and saw that I was comfortable, which, as it was late at night and I had never been in Manchester before, was a very good thing for me. It's no fun for a grown man to be stranded in a strange place like that, let alone a young lad.

My first regular job on the cars was with the Glasgow portion of the 2 o'clock, which used to be called the 'Corridor' because it was the only train regularly formed of corridor stock; and even then we would sometimes find a non-corridor [This LNWR express was often formed badly like this, possibly due to carelessness on the part of the shunters who would have been unfamiliar with corridor rolling stock, but it would also have been due to a shortage of rolling stock if something was faulty with one of the 'new-fangled' corridor carriages. The sensible way would have been to put the non-corridor carriage near the end, but especially on a portioned working such as this, there were some rigid rules to be observed about where each class of carriage would be placed] vehicle put right in the centre, cutting off part of the train from the car and causing no end of complaints! I think that at that time, too, the 'Corridor' was the only train with third-class dining cars.

I believe it was in July 1899, that the 10.00am was made a corridor train too, and for some time I travelled with that, until one day, on returning from my holidays, I was told I was not to go back, as it had been decided to promote me. I was then just 21 years old. Promotion did not come at once, however, and meanwhile I had to go 'spare', which meant taking any old job that came along, such as a 'Yankee' special [At this time, the North Atlantic liners used Liverpool as their English port, and the 'Yankee special' was a boat train which would only run on those occasions when a liner called], for instance, or one of the extra cars frequently wanted on the 5.30pm. When there was nothing else to do we cleaned the silver in stock.

It was on arrival at Liverpool with a 'Yankee' that I at last got instructions to take up my new job. They took the form of a wire telling me to return to London as a passenger at once so as to be ready for the Aberdeen train next morning; and from that day my wages were increased to the princely sum of one sovereign weekly!

The next few years of my life were principally spent in Scotland, where I was stationed in various places. We worked some long hours then. I remember one circuit on which we started from Aberdeen at 6.00am and did not get back until 10.15 at night; and there was another funny circuit worked by two men and a boy, and we men took it turn and turn about to be senior, each working one day as 'boy'. The boy? Oh, he was a boy all the time, of course, and, as you may imagine, he had to work hard for his living.

Breakages? Well, yes, you are bound to get a certain number even when the cars run as smoothly as ours; but the finest smash I ever saw was years ago, when everything in the car was broken – bottles of wine and all. It happened like this. The engine which was to have pulled us out of the siding up to the platform took the wrong turning and ran into the stops instead. As luck would have it, all the tables were fully laid for lunch, and the bump simply shot the lot on to the floor. It was a lovely mess, I can tell you – looked like a rubbish heap! I was in the pantry at the time, just going to wash up, and was thrown right across the compartment into the sink, saturating my clothes. Most fortunately, the little window above it which communicates with the kitchen was open, for my head was forced through it; had the glass sash been down, I shudder to think what might have happened.

As it was, however, I escaped with nothing worse than a severe shaking and a strong desire never to be in an accident again.

It is wonderful how well the arrangements for stocking the cars work out. I never remember any serious difficulty through failure in this way – except once, when the cook found out after we had started that he was badly short of pots. However, we got over it by using biscuit tins; everything went well and we never said anything about it. No, I'm not going to tell you when or where it happened!

I think that we generally manage to give satisfaction. The public always seem to enjoy their meals. Of course, sometimes we get people with special fads, but if they want a special dinner, not on our ordinary menu, it is ordered at Euston beforehand, and, of course, we are prepared. I recollect an Indian Rajah who used to have curries and such-like dishes specially prepared for him. We always knew when he was going to travel, so there was no trouble; but I often think of the consternation of his staff one day when the cushions happened to be of leather. There was a great rush about to find a cloth to put between his person and the seat. I suppose he would have lost caste if he had touched cowhide, but I couldn't help smiling to myself because I believe the upholstery was really a very fine imitation, and not genuine hide at all! However, it's best not to take risks, isn't it? Safety first, always.

The Americans are amusing. They get through the cutlery very quickly, often using more than one knife and fork for a course, so their [sic] without either long before dinner's over. And they very often use one hand only, cutting up first and eating after!

Another thing they don't understand is the red-currant jelly we eat with roat mutton. I remember once seeing one take an enormous helping on his plate and eat it up after finishing the meat, spread like jam. He evidently liked it, for when cheese was served he called for a second helping of the jelly!

I have had some queer cards on my staff too. I remember one man who tried to grill boiled potatoes and another – during the early part of the war, it was – who thought bright stars were Zeppelins, and I had great difficulty in preventing him from alarming passengers!

There is no doubt about it, that the restaurant car, which used to be regarded as a luxury, is becoming more and more a necessity for railway travel. You have only to compare the two West Coast cars seating a total of sixteen firsts and eighteen thirds manned by one conductor, two kitchen staff and three boys, which used to run on the old 'Corridor' with the reduced winter accommodation on the 'Royal Scot' today – the Edinburgh car with fifteen first and twenty-one third-class seats, and the Glasgow with its wonderful kitchen car and vestibule coaches seating thirty-six firsts and forty-two third, the whole requiring three conductors, three kitchen staff and eight boys.

It speaks for itself, doesn't it – and mind, that's only one train, and a 'winter' service into the bargain; it's far heavier in the summer time. My own humble opinion is that so long as we work to the motto on the 'Royal Scot' menu, 'Heich abune the heich', which my good assistant from Aberdeen me means 'Best amongst the best' – (I'm no Scottish scholar myself, so we must take his word for it!) – our business will go on increasing, and other companies will have their work cut out to touch the LMS.

A remarkable period of service, and one that spanned not just two centuries but trains of very different periods.

Chapter 7

Night Mail and Newspapers

One task that was awarded to the railways almost from the beginning was that of carrying the mails, and this was so important that Parliament very shortly afterwards gave the Post Office the right to insist on provision being made for mail to be carried by train. At first, mail was simply delivered to the train and taken off at its destination, but the practice of onboard sorting emerged as early as 1838 between Birmingham and Liverpool on the Grand Junction Railway, and continued until relatively recently except for the Second World War when it was suspended. The trains were under the control of the Post Office.

Another overnight high priority traffic was the newspapers, and in addition to carrying newspapers on passenger trains, there were a large number of trains specifically dedicated to this important traffic.

Night Mail

All of the 'Big Four' main line companies operated mail trains, and on the Great Western the longest distance was for 312 miles from Paddington to Penzance. This account was written by one R.F. Thurtle, who was given special permission by the Post Office to travel on the train, and appeared in *The Great Western Railway Magazine*, which he edited at the time. Carriages in which sorting took place as opposed to those that simply carried the mail through to its destination were known as travelling post offices, or TPOs.

> The train consisted of five coaches specialised for Post Office work (lettered 'A' to 'E'), a brake van, and two 'Siphons G' [Large vans for parcels and packages], was hauled into Paddington station at 8.45pm and mails soon began to arrive in large quantities. Most of these were trolleyed across from the Paddington station outlet of the Post Office Tube Railway, where the delivery belt was spouting forth a continuous stream of the familiar grey canvas bags.

Thousands of these, of all shapes and sizes, were steadily received and stowed into the train. Each bag from the Post Office tube bore two distinctive labels, one the Paddington station label (for the guidance of GPO tube train stowers) and the other either a label through to a destination station or to the Great Western TPO. In accordance with these labels the bags were stowed in one or the other of the coaches. It was soon obvious that the two 'siphons' were intended for through parcel mails only, one for Bristol and the other for Exeter, and that these vehicles had no interest for the sorters, some of whom were on duty and busy at their work soon after the train was in position at the platform.

Punctually at 10.10pm the train steamed out of Paddington, and the courteous overseer-in-charge (Mr J.D. Leahy) was able to put his passenger in the way of seeing what was going on. The personnel of the TPO was about twenty-five. Five sorters would work through to Truro, eight to Bristol, and the remainder to Plymouth, where additional staff would join the train for completion of the Cornish sorting.

The interiors of the coaches are definitely utilitarian in character. One side of each vehicle is equipped with numbered hooks for hanging the mail bags, and the other side with counters and numbered sorting racks or boxes. These are of two kinds – one designed for letters and the other for the 'news' mail. For sorting purposes the 'news' category includes all large packages that are conveyed at letter rate.

Sections of counter in each coach are allocated to the recording and sorting of registered letters, as well as for the overseer's use. The coaches also have special accommodation in the form of cupboards that can be locked.

The actual sorting of letters is carried out in a series of 'plans'. These are groups of fifty-four boxes, or, more precisely, five rows of nine boxes and one row of nine partitions on the surface of the counter. These plans can be duplicated for any given territory, as may be necessary to get the work accomplished to time. Generally speaking, the places represented in the 'plans' are memorised by the sorters, but occasionally some of the place names are chalked on the racks in an abbreviated form.

Work first to be disposed of is known as 'the immediate', and has preference over all other. There was every evidence of a good team spirit in the TPO, and of commendable concentration on the job in hand. Conversation among the sorters was fragmentary and mainly concerned the elucidation of doubtful addresses, but even that was so swiftly done as hardly to impede the torrent of letters speeding home. When a good number of letters had been sorted for separate destinations they were bundled and dropped into the appropriate bags, whereupon the sorting process was continued on fresh supplies.

Every mail bag made up in the TPO is sealed by passing a small tube of lead over the strings after tieing, and compressing the lead with a sealing punch. The bags are also boldly labelled as from the Great Western Down TPO to their destinations. Including the bundling of letters, tieing and sealing of bags and other incidental work, it is estimated letters are disposed of by each sorter at an average rate of thirty per minute.

For the sorting of the 'news', a type of larger boxes is used, and by reason of this and variety of the mail the process is slower than with letters.

Quite a good deal of recording has to be done by the overseer-in-charge of the Travelling Post Office. One of his nightly records is almost a facsimile of a passenger guard journal, with booked and actual times and space for explanation of any delay. But the most important document is an elaborate and comprehensive one which bears the title of 'tick sheet'. On this is a printed a complete record of mail bags to be received and despatched from the TPO, the checking and 'ticking' of which doubtless gives the document its name. There is also a space on the 'tick sheet' for every member of the TPO staff to sign on and off duty. The principal basis for compiling this important record is the 'bag bill', a small sheet which is enclosed with every mail bag received. So, if the bag bill has been received, so, undoubtedly, has the bag. Mails reach the Paddington–Penzance TPO from all parts of the country and also from abroad, several bags being received each night from Germany. Each shows places of origin and destination for each bag, and gives particulars of any registered letters it may contain. When registered letters are at all numerous they are separately bagged and are in all cases specially safeguarded.

The duties of the Travelling Post Office staff are not very rigidly specialised, although they are organised in definite 'cycles'.

Members of the junior 'cycle' undertake stipulated duties, including operation of the exchange apparatus, and more advanced 'cycles' embrace general sorting, registered letter work, etc. Moreover, in the actual sorting a man does not always handle letters for the same district, i.e. Somerset, Devon or Cornwall, but covers in turn all the duties allotted to his particular 'cycle' and thus obtains familiarity with the work as a whole.

The mail exchange apparatus, as is generally known, is a means of putting out and picking up mails while the train is in motion. Mails dispatched and received by apparatus are encased in strong leather pouches, as they sustain a considerable impact on every exchange. The pouches each weigh 20-lb unladen, and when operated must not exceed 60-lb, including their load of mails. Briefly, the apparatus works in this way. There is carried on the outer side of the apparatus coach a *mail-catching* net which, upon a lever being lowered in the coach, is thrust out so as to dislodge and catch pouches which have previously been hung on 'arms' from a rail-side frame. This *receiving* apparatus is at a fairly high level in the coach.

The *dispatching* apparatus operates the same kind of mechanism in the reverse order. That is to say, the 'arms' are in the coach (at the doors), and the net is outside by the rail side. The dispatching 'arms' are near the coach floor, the pouches actually hanging well below that level. This provision enables mails to be received and dispatched at the same time without obstruction.

An important factor in mail apparatus work is the timely location of exchange posts. These carry special lights, as do the apparatus coaches, but additional means of location are necessary, and these may be of various kinds. White boards are usually provided at the rail side, while the TPO operator also has his own preliminary indications when approaching an exchange post.

An enthusiastic young sorter was in charge of the apparatus on the occasion of the writer's journey. As he stood, keenly alert, at the door of the coach, with his fair hair flying in the wind, he looked a romantic figure. For one of his exchanges this was his formula: 'Pass the station, pass the signal-box, and after the third bridge lower the lever.' This mental recital, together with the confirmation provided by the white board, made his timing perfect.

The lever was, of course, restored to 'normal' immediately an exchange had been effected. When four pouches had to be dropped at one place, necessitating the use of both doors of the coach, the operator called in the assistance of a colleague to swing out two of the pouches.

When an exchange is in progress it is desirable to stand well clear of the net, as the pouches bounce into the coach with a very lively 'kick'. A bell is rung to warn the staff. There is a queer illusion in watching a mail exchange for the first time. When two pouches go and two arrive almost simultaneously, an observer gets the odd impression that the same pair have swung back in again – except, of course, that neither the Great Western Railway nor the General Post Office could do anything so foolish.

On the 10.10pm Paddington to Penzance mail train apparatus exchanges are made at Slough, Maidenhead, Wantage Road, Swindon, Chippenham, Bridgwater, St Germans, Liskeard, Lostwithiel, Redruth and Cambourne. A note of Great Western interest in connection with the mail exchange apparatus, which so excellently serves its purpose, is that the last improvements effected (that was over thirty years ago) were suggested by a Great Western Railway Swindon mechanic ... who afterwards joined the Post Office service and specialised in training staff for mail apparatus work.

The number of bags dealt with in the Paddington–Penzance TPO varies very little, but with the actual quantity of mail it is entirely different. Not only are some nights much heavier than others, Mondays and Fridays being notably busy. But the incidence of month-end and quarter-end also materially affects the volume of letters. Direct mail conveyed, that is, bags labelled through to their destination, vastly exceeds the mails actually sorted in the TPO.

It was quite thrilling to watch the important part played by express railway transport in the speedy transmission of letters, and also to be able to appreciate at first hand what an organised hive of industry is the 10.10pm Paddington to Penzance Travelling Post Office.

This was clearly a 'mail-only' train as many TPOs were attached to passenger expressed such as the 'Irish Mail', for example.

A Night with the News

By coincidence, this also came from the *The Great Western Railway Magazine* and its roaming editor, R.F. Thurtle, and although on this occasion the GWR was in charge of the train, unlike the mail trains, he did not travel with the newspapers. It should be mentioned, when looking at the timings, that at the time the number of regional morning newspapers was far higher than today, and so too was their circulation, so many in the GWR area would have been reading the Bristol *Western Morning Post* or the Plymouth *Western Morning News*, for example. This in part justifies what seems like a very late arrival at Penzance.

> The morning newspaper ranks high amongst the necessities of modern civilisation. Even the broadcasting of news bulletins by wireless has not seriously affected its importance, and it is safe to say that the national influence of the newspaper was never more potent than now. The paper comes to us at breakfast time with an exemplary regularity, and incidentally has a widespread reputation for eliminating conversation from the morning meal ... What are the transport arrangements by which this regular and almost unfailing arrival is secured?
>
> South Wales, the West and the West Midlands are the principal areas to which newspapers are despatched from Paddington, and two special trains are entirely devoted to their conveyance. The 1.40am runs as a newspaper train to Plymouth North Road via the Lavington route, having Taunton as its first stop. From Plymouth journey is continued as a passenger train, Penzance being reached at 8.48am.
>
> The 2.30am is the newspaper train for Bristol, and regularly conveys traffic for a wide area served from that point, as well as vans detached en route, which serve Oxford, Swindon, Gloucester and the surrounding districts. On Monday mornings this train covers, in addition, the South Wales traffic, which usually occupies four large vans. These are worked through from Bristol to Swansea, leaving the former point at 4.55am and giving a sufficiently early arrival at destination points in South Wales. On other mornings of the week the South Wales traffic is conveyed by the 12.55am mail train.

There is also, as will be appreciated, a heavy newspaper traffic from Paddington to stations in the suburbs and Home Counties, but this is despatched by early morning passenger trains.

It was round about midnight on a Sunday that I went to Paddington for the purpose of seeing the papers come and go ... a steady stream of news-laden motor vans made the turn into Paddington Station approach road.

There were the vans of the *Daily Mail*, ample and obvious, in brilliant red lettering on a yellow ground. No hiding of *their* light in a bushel. The *Daily Express* arrived, mainly in the red vans, familiar to Londoners, of the *Evening Standard*, although one or two *Express* vehicles were to be seen, in striking green and yellow dress. Chocolate is the hue which distinguishes *Daily Mirror* vans, the work being assisted by their Sunday associate, the *Pictorial*, in vans of like colour. The *Daily Sketch* favours orange.

On arrival of the vans at Paddington they were 'backed' into position by the drivers who also throw the doors open, after which the company's porters commence their duties. It should be said that vans containing traffic for the 1.40am train (berthed on No. 4 platform) are driven to a convenient position on 'the lawn' [The title, still in use today, by which railwaymen know the main concourse at Paddington], while those with traffic for the 2.30am (berthed at No. 1 platform) are dealt with on the departure road.

Literally, dozens of four-wheeled trolleys are placed ready to receive the parcels of papers, and the unloading of the vans is rapidly accomplished, the vans thereby released for subsequent journeys to and from the printing works. The parcels vary in size and weight, but are usually substantial ones, averaging about 30-lb. The labels are largely standardised in size and form, and have all relevant particulars clearly and heavily printed. In particular, the destination station is always in large and heavy type, and where necessary, also, a route indication is given.

By reason of the traffic being regular, it is possible for the consignees' names to be printed. Another simple expedient, designed for convenience at the destination station, is to print labels for different consignees in the same town on differently coloured paper, the danger of errors in delivery being thus substantially minimised. Particulars which the labels usually indicate are: name of newspaper; consignee's name; destination station; route, where necessary; number of quires in parcel; and the conditions of conveyance, i.e. carriage paid – by ledger account or contract. In addition, there is a system of indicating, by means of distinctive letters on the labels, groups into which the parcels have to be sorted.

When the four-wheeled trolleys have been filled from the arriving motor vans the papers are hauled away for weighing, stowing and recording. Stowing is accomplished by experienced men, who know by instruction and experience the sides and 'spots' of the respective vans which meet the convenience of the staff at receiving stations. The importance of order and consistency in stowing cannot be exaggerated. Considerable loss, both of time and temper, would otherwise be inevitable.

Weighing and recording are carried out in accordance with instructions. Not every parcel of newspapers is weighed every night. That is not necessary in view of the contract arrangements, nor would it be easily practicable. A high degree of cooperation has been achieved between the newspaper proprietors and the Company's officers, as a result of which accountancy, in common with other phases of newspaper conveyance, is smoothly and efficiently carried through. In ever newspaper van a weighing balance is provided, and several clerks are available at Paddington for record purposes. Two clerks, together with porters, travel on the 2.30am train as far as Swindon to enable the required records to be satisfactorily completed.

A feature which struck me most favourably in connection with the newspaper traffic at Paddington was the absence of noise and confusion in carrying out the work. Organisation was apparent everywhere, and each man seemed to know just what was expected of him. There was no sign of nocturnal drowsiness, but the comparative quiet with which the work was done seemed fully in harmony with the hour.

The inspector on duty was ubiquitous; here, there, and always on his job, with papers in hand and a quiet but apparently effective word for many of the staff. He did not speak to me, but I enjoyed a minor thrill when the railway policeman did! Politely, and very properly (for why should a stranger in mufti be dodging about Paddington at two in the morning?) he asked me if I was travelling. Then we made friends, but it was good to have thus proved that the Company's police are keen about their business, and not merely decorative.

On the night of my visit the whole of the day's papers had reached the station in reasonable time, but sometimes when a late and important news item has come through, the presses are kept running later than usual, with the result that time is more than ever precious at Paddington.

Special trains have from time to time been chartered, either by reason of domestic circumstances at one or other of the great newspaper presses, or on account of news too momentous to wait. Such occasions have occurred in the past and inevitably must occur in the future. Whenever the need may arise the railways may be depended upon, and will not be found wanting.

Chapter 8

In the Shed

The locomotive shed was very much behind the scenes, and not always the best place to be, being filthy and full of smoke, even though the disposal of ash from the locomotive firebox would have taken place outside, and so too would coaling before returning to service. Many sheds were poorly maintained, with strong draughts in winter and rain water leaking through the roof. The impoverished railways between the two world wars did build new sheds and reorganise those inherited from the pre-grouping companies, but while standardisation within each of the 'Big Four' was important, there were many other demands for new investment.

Grouping gave some of the companies major problems in standardising working practices, which was bad enough, but there could be design features from the assembled locomotives designed by different chief mechanical engineers and built at different locations. No better example of the problems was the fact that former LNWR and Midland steam locomotives had regulators that worked in the opposite directions. The Midland practice was the standard for most railways, and when an ex-Midland driver found himself in a former LNWR steam locomotive cab, he had to remember that the regulator worked in the opposite direction. Many forgot, and locomotives ended up being reversed through the shed wall of a roundhouse. This might have been understandable, but were in addition to many cases of carelessness when locomotives were run into the turntable well, which put the shed out of action for several hours.

One of the more dramatic items of equipment belonging to the shed was actually outside it in the sidings, the breakdown crane. These were scattered around the country to minimise the delay in reaching an accident or derailment.

Working *with* an Accident Crane

One of the busiest sheds on the LNER was at Stratford, with the busy commuter services out of Liverpool Street, and the account of the work of the breakdown or accident crane comes from the *London & North Eastern Railway Magazine*, written by Frank Wilson, who worked in the District Locomotive Superintendent's Office.

'Variety is the spice of life.' So wrote one of the sages, and if this be true, the life of a breakdown crew must be ideal, for it is made up of variety. Accidents happen in the best-regulated families, and the railway family is no exception to this rule. Mishaps – some serious, others not – occur at times, and may vary from the derailment of a large engine at a busy place where there is nothing more solid to work on than a spider-web of point rods and signal wires, to a truck of cabbages inverted in a ditch at some wayside station. Whatever may happen a breakdown train is sent quickly in order to minimise delay, and in cases of mishaps to passenger trains the prompt arrival of the breakdown equipment may easily be the means of saving life or limb. The train and crew – the first-aid service, as it were, of operations – must therefore be available at short notice, and the following brief account shows what is done at Stratford, where one of the cranes ... is stationed.

The boiler of the crane is kept continuously in steam, and the crew must, like medical men, be prepared to turn out at any time during the day or night. During working hours the men are spread around the shed on their normal duties, and are readily collected when there is a call for the breakdown train – or accident van, as it is sometimes called. Most of the men who make up the complement of the train live close to the works in houses connected to the running shed by electric bells or gongs similar to those used in signal boxes, and after working hours these gongs are used to summon the men. The foreman is advised by telephone and given particulars of the mishap, while the running foreman arranges for an engine to work the train, and the Control Office (which has requested the train) provides a guard, the whole usually being ready to start within a very few minutes. After leaving the running shed, the train is treated and signalled as an 'express' and the line is cleared as fast as possible for its passage to the scene of trouble. This, in short, is what happens behind the scenes when we read in our newspapers a lurid account of how 'a breakdown gang was feverishly rushed to the scene of disaster.'

The crane is capable of lifting a load of 35 tons and weighs 80 tons, carried on ten wheels. Steam is generated in a water-tube boiler working at a pressure of 100-lb per square inch, and, if necessary, the crane can travel short distances under its own power. When running, the jib is, of course, down on the guard truck, and, despite its bulk and seeming clumsiness, the crane can be hauled in safety as fast as an ordinary passenger train. An electric generator driven by steam from the boiler provides current to light the cab of the crane as well as two large lamps fixed at the end of the jib, enabling objects which have to be lifted at night to be illuminated perfectly. In addition to the crane and guard trucks there is a brake van conveying lifting jacks and the thousand-and-one tools and accessories likely to be required, and lastly, a bogie van arranged for the comfort of the staff. The staff usually consists of a crane-driver, a fitter and seven other men, with a foreman in charge, but when serious accidents occur some of the company's officers travel in this vehicle, and a separate compartment is provided for them. As the train is sometimes away from the depot for several hours at a stretch, sufficient food and water is carried to last for 24 hours, and a stove and cooking utensils are supplied.

The use of the crane is not confined to clearing up mishaps, and frequently there are engineering works in hand requiring powerful cranes for lifting out old bridges or for placing new girder-work in position. Very often two such cranes are required for large jobs [as when] the Stratford and King's Cross cranes engaged in lifting heavy plate girders at the Minories, just outside Fenchurch Street station, London, where extensive reconstruction work is in progress ... The work occupied about thirty hours, and the trough flooring of the old bridge ... had to be suspended by the crane and cut away by means of oxyacetylene plant ...

Last year at Southend the Stratford crane was put to a novel use at the Railway Exhibition [The LNER used to stage railway exhibitions at major points in its network, showing new loco-motives and both passenger and goods rolling stock, and often complementing these with preserved equipment as well, keen to show that it could trace its ancestry back to the Stockton &

Darlington Railway], where it proved extremely popular with thousands of visitors and helped to swell the contribution to charity. It was ... used as an aerial roundabout: an old truck (padded inside) was suspended from the jib, and for a small charge about forty people at a time were lifted well up from the ground, swung around in a complete circle, and again lowered to terra firma.

Clearly, these were the days before the Health & Safety mafia ruled.

Working *without* an Accident Crane

In Chapter 16 we come across Alistair MacLeod as he tackles the railways on the Isle of Wight, which just six years earlier had been three different companies running on track owned by five different companies. The Ryde to Ventnor line was the busiest, but Newport was the centre of the island's transport system and as Ryde was the main port for passengers, he was based there. With a system that was largely single tracked, any untoward event was more difficult to handle than on the mainland, and even the so-called 'main lines' were in effect just busy branches, single tracked with passing loops, so that derailments or accidents could be difficult to reach.

In the winter of 1928, my first on the island, I was rung up one evening and advised that there had been a derailment at Wroxall of the 8.43pm train ex-Ventnor and would I come. A few minutes later Bob Sweetman phoned me to say that several coaches were tangled up at Wroxall owing to a broken gauge glass on locomotive No. W23.

We took the Ryde breakdown tool van up to Shanklin but as the single line was occupied to Wroxall, the van and engine had to stop there. We put some jacks and packing in Bob's bull-nosed Morris touring car and, with a fitter and mate, proceeded by road and found a 'right tangle up'.

As W23 was entering the south end of the loop line at Wroxall, a boiler gauge-glass burst, filling the cab with steam. The driver threw his coat over the broken gauge-glass and endeavoured to shut the regulator and apply the emergency brake, while the fireman put on the handbrake but unfortunately the engine had passed the starting signal at 'danger' and by then had gone two coach lengths beyond the north end of the loop before coming to a stand, splitting the points, which were set for the down track and fouling the down home signal in the process. The fireman had by then been able to shut off the gauge cocks under the driver's coat.

The driver then, not fully realising the position, released the brakes, reversed his engine and opened the regulator to set the train back into the up platform ... You can imagine what happened then; the second coach spread-eagled at right angles and the first coach and W23 tried to go into the down road, and as the train was close-coupled, no couplings gave way and movement came to a sudden halt. But this was not all the trouble as it transpired that the 8.43pm train ex-Ventnor was running late and in order not to delay the 8.20pm from Ryde Pier Head. Which was normally due to cross the up train at Shanklin, the signalman had advised Shanklin to let the down train proceed with a view to crossing at Wroxall instead.

So while all this drama of W23 was going on, the down train, with another O2 class engine, was pounding up Apse Bank towards Wroxall and might have struck the wreckage as the down home signal had been lowered. The fireman of W23 saved the day by running down the bank and placing fog signals on the track so stopped the train from Shanklin but it was quite a near thing.

Luckily there were no passengers in the first two coaches of the up train and so no complaints were made except for bad jolting to the people in the last six coaches when the train finally stopped. The few passengers in both trains were sent forward by taxis, which had been summoned from Ventnor. The down train was sent back empty to Shanklin and the breakdown van sent up. We had to cut through the long coupling links with the oxyacetylene cutter in order to free the leading four wheelers before effecting re-railment with the jacks. It took till 6am to clear the line and repair the points, and the mails, instead of going through to Ventnor on the 4.00am train from Pier Head, had to be transferred to a lorry at Shanklin.

MacLeod noted that they were fortunate that the conditions were dry. Inevitably, there was an enquiry, although all Macleod says was that there were some awards and some chastisements. One hopes that the fireman of W23 came out well, but one can have some sympathy for the predicament of the driver of the locomotive, although he should have checked its position before attempting to reverse.

While this was the worst derailment that he experienced, while on the island there were a number of collisions at level crossings. One of these was when a locomotive running from Cowes to Newport collided with a cement lorry. This mustn't have been too serious as the locomotive was not derailed, but it did arrive at Newport covered in cement powder, '... pure white from buffer beam to tail light.'

The Labourer

In 1930, the then editor of the *Great Western Railway Magazine*, Edward Hadley, made a point of gaining what he called first-hand knowledge of the many tasks on the railway, not so much to gain a broad knowledge of the railway itself, but to compile practical handbooks on accident prevention. This and the ambulance classes sponsored by the GWR were a persistent theme in the magazine. Other railway company magazines also ran photographs showing how to and how not to do something, such as not walking on the track, or standing on buffers when coupling wagons.

For this particular exercise he was officially described as a labourer and given the number of 210, although his new workmates called him Dick. 'Labourer' is probably not the term that would be used today, as he spent time as a plumber's mate before working for a brass finisher on locks and for a tinsmith. Hadley normally wrote in the third person when on these 'learning' exercises.

His hours of work were from 7.30am to 5.00pm, with an hour, 12.00 to 1.00, for dinner. Although the timekeeper is said to follow the second-hand of his watch when the men are 'booking in', the editor managed to escape being 'stopped half an hour' for lateness on any morning. He found the forenoons long, and was always thankful when the 'hooter' sounded dinner-time. Then, along with his mates, he went to the mess room where 'Old Topper', the cook, invariably had a pint of tea waiting for him. The mess room was clean, warm, and well ventilated, and everyone was friendly and jocular. After the meal there was just time for a pipe before the 'hooter for the boss' called the men back to 'the job'.

The editor started at the depot as plumber's mate, and 'Charlie', the plumber, soon initiated him into the aches and pains from hours of hammering to straighten bent and dented lead pipes. 'Charlie' had on the bench a length of about 20 feet of 2-inch lead pipe. In it were dents and curves enough, as one man said, 'to break your heart', but 'Charlie' declared that this pipe was really 'a picture' compared to what some of them were. The job was to drive a hardwood egg-shaped block, 2 inches in diameter, through the entire length of the pipe, using a mallet and rods. 'Charlie' gave 'Dick' the mallet and himself 'supervised' the work, and whenever there was a particularly deep dent to be encountered, taxing every ounce of the editor's strength, there was the merriest of twinkles in 'Charlie's' eye.

If that day's work was a fair specimen of a plumber's toil, no wonder that the plumber's mate contrives now and then 'to forget the tools' so as to gain some respite in going back to fetch them!

After the plumbing, the editor went to another bench in the shop, as mate to 'Harry', the brass finisher. Mending locks of various types and cutting new keys were the chief jobs here; but 'Harry', who was the embodiment of good-nature, went out of his way to enlighten 'Dick' upon several processes and operations.

In the same shop was 'Ernie', the tinsmith – a quiet, cultured, clever fellow, who took a great interest in the editor's quest, and did all he could to be helpful.

And just as much as in this, the editor's first shop, there was in all the other shops, and in the yard outside, a readiness to assist.

Hmm, obviously all good fellows!

The Cleaners

One of the most basic and filthy jobs on the railways was that of the engine cleaner, but this was the starting point for anyone who wanted to become an engine driver. Cleaners had to be 'passed' as competent before they could hope to fill a vacancy as a fireman, and in turn be 'passed' firemen before they could hope to drive a locomotive. Even then, there was a hierarchy and it would be many years before they could find themselves in the top link, that select band who handled the famous expresses or even royal trains.

G.C. Potts, in his book, *Bankers & Pilots* [See glossary for explanation of these terms] *Footplate Memories*, recalls starting as an engine cleaner, working at Mexborough shed on what was then still the Great Central

Railway in December 1922, less than three weeks before it became part
of the London & North Eastern Railway.

> For cleaning, we all congregated outside the foreman cleaner's
> room. In seniority order, gangs of four men were given a loco-
> motive to clean with two dozen sponge cloths and one dozen
> soaked in oil. If you were cleaning a passenger loco, you would
> also have a tin of white paste, which was to preserve the paint-
> work. Paraffin had to be used occasionally on the wheels.
> When you arrived at the loco, a coin was tossed for partners if
> you hadn't come to a decision beforehand. Next, the partners
> would toss once more to divide the work – tops and paints, which
> were the boiler, smokebox, cabside and tender bottom, or the
> remainder, that is the wheels and tender side. If the foreman said
> the motion had to be cleaned, each pair tossed against the other,
> the losers doing the motion, the other two the rest. The passenger
> locomotives, of which we had some fourteen, including tanks,
> were cleaned every day and I might add that they looked splendid
> – brass work polished up and special black oil for the smokebox
> … Each of these locomotives was allocated to a driver [A practice
> that eventually disappeared and drivers drove any locomotive
> allocated to them.] who jealously wanted it when it was available.
> As a cleaner you were also a utility man and could be used for any
> kind of job on the premises, emptying ash pits, filling wagons
> with ashes, filling tubs on the coal stage, emptying sand wagons
> into the sand furnace hopper, informing firemen and drivers at
> their homes of any alteration in their rostered working during the
> day and knocking up during the night if any one of the knockers-
> up failed to come on duty; most of the latter were partially dis-
> abled or could not do manual work. This duty for the cleaner
> earned extra money but it was hard-earned, too, tramping round
> the streets in all kinds of weather so as not to call up the men
> before it was time.

This was a demanding role, filthy work and today it would be regarded as unhealthy, requiring special clothing over and above the
dungarees and jacket worn. Between the wars, some of the work was
mechanised, notably the filling of the coal tubs, which would have
been replaced by coaling towers, although these were impractical for
tank engines.

Potts stuck at the cleaning job for two years, before applying for a vacancy as a fire-bar layer, which became available when the previous incumbent was promoted to spare fireman. In this role he had another cleaner as partner so that when one was in the firebox, the other would be watching to ensure that he was safe. It was not until 1927 that the 1922 intake was regarded as being suitable for promotion to firemen, for which they had first to undergo study at the improvement classes because the fireman on a locomotive had to be able to react if the driver was taken ill, and help him in looking out for signals, as well as handling couplings, brake pipes, lamps, refilling the water tanks in the tenders at a water tower or handling the scoop to pick up water whilst on the move, and, of course, he had to keep the fire fed and yet not overdo it and waste coal, especially at the end of the day's work.

Another driver who started as a cleaner was N. Dixon, whose account of his railway years appeared in his book *A Yorkshire Locoman – LNER Memories*, which appeared in 1983. He seemed to have been promoted to fireman after just six months as a cleaner, but he still reverted to cleaner when no firing turns were available, and some of the jobs were decidedly unpleasant and arduous.

> … on one or two occasions when an engine was reported steaming badly, was to sweep the tubes out. This was a very dirty business; often the fire had been left in and smoke and fumes were blowing at me as I worked. When you think that there were up to three hundred tubes in a larger engine, it meant a long hard job to get them clean. First you pushed a long rod through to get the hard soot off and then, if there was a compressor in the shed, you blew the tubes through with compressed air. Having no compressor at Haverton Hill, we had to fit the blower on to a water gauge fitting and blow the tubes though with steam. Using this made the job warmer than it should have been, of course. In those days cleaners had to do this kind of work but received no extra pay for doing so; the custom was that if a cleaner did a full day's labouring he was allowed to go home one hour earlier. But on the coal stage I had to work through and take food as and when I could because the coal stage men put in a straight eight hours without a break!

So much for the romance of the steam age.

A Day in the Running Shed

This comes from the early 1920s, when the *London & North Eastern Railway Magazine* was still known as the *North Eastern & Scottish Magazine* – it took some railways longer than others to adapt to grouping and the North Eastern was the dominant constituent company of the LNER for some time. The article is based on a day in York shed, one of the most important if not the most important on the LNER, but again, NER dominance tells.

It does give a very thorough background to the behind the scenes work in keeping a railway running, and shows just how intensive was the work needed to be done to keep steam locomotives in good working order, even if, under duress, such as wartime conditions, they could take considerably more abuse and neglect than a diesel. The details of coaling show it to be dated as the coaling towers that came in to widespread use between the wars are referred to as a '... more modern method.' It is also interesting that no mention is made of water softening as many railways introduced such equipment both for the water towers at stations and yards and, of course, for the water troughs which enabled locomotives to pick up water whilst travelling at speed.

Written under the pen-name of 'Headlamp', the piece was in two parts and altogether took some six pages, extensively illustrated, which shows either how involved was the subject, or how the NER at this stage still got its own way. The first part dealt with preparation of the locomotive for its day's work, and largely duplicates the story told later by the locomotive driver at Stratford.

> Having completed its trip, the engine on its return to the shed passes by the coal stage, where the tender is filled up with coal and water. As much as 5 tons of coal has sometimes to be supplied. The coal tubs, each holding about 10 cwt, have been filled from the wagons on the elevated stage, and are tipped into a shoot, where the coal slides down on to the tender. A more modern method is to have the coal stored in large elevated hoppers. The engines stop underneath, and the required amount of coal is dropped through an opening in the bottom of the hopper. The daily issue of coal at a large shed is between 300 and 400 tons.

The trainmen are relieved by another set of enginemen for stabling after arrival in the shed yard. Before booking off at the time office, the engine driver enters in the report book any defects he has found in the running of the engine. He has also to make out his voucher, giving a detailed account of the day's work.

The stabling set who have taken charge of the engine, bring it on to the stabling pit, where they rake out the ashpan, lift all the scar and ashes out of the firebox, and empty the black ash out of the smokebox. The engine is then brought into the shed, and turned off into a stall, where the fireman replenishes the sand-boxes, and takes the lamps to the stores to be retrimmed. The stabling driver meanwhile examines the engine for defects. It is again in the hands of the shed staff to get ready for its next trip.

After about every seventh trip the boiler must be washed out to clear it of sediment. This sediment accumulates by the water being converted into steam, leaving in the boiler all dirt and salts it may have contained. The amount varies in districts. The dirt, clinging to the tubes and firebox, prevents the full transmission of heat from the fire to the water, with consequent loss of efficiency. The salts in solution become concentrated, and cause priming. To save coal and keep the engine at full power, it is essential that the boiler be kept clean. Prior to washing out, all the steam is blown off, and the boiler allowed to cool down. This cooling must not be done quickly, as if rapidly cooled, severe strains would be set up through unequal contraction, causing leakage of water at the tubes and seems. Every time a boiler is washed out, it is examined by a boiler-smith for defects in the plates, tubes and stays. The fusible plugs in the firebox crown are to prevent damage to the plates by a shortage of water. They require frequent renewal, as when they deteriorate with the intense heat of the fire, they are liable to fail when the engine is in traffic [i.e. working], and disable it, although there still might be an ample supply of water in the boiler. A record is kept of all these examinations and renewals. When washed out with cold water, the engine is of necessity out of service for a considerable time. This time is reduced by 60 per cent if hot water apparatus is used. The gain in time, and the less maintenance required with hot water washing out is a great advantage. A service of pipes is laid around the shed, and these in turn are coupled to the boiler to be washed out.

The hot water is run through a pipe to the tank, and filtered. Hot water is pumped into the boiler through the service pipes to wash it out, and finally the boiler is filled with hot water, and steam can be very rapidly raised. This gain in time is so great that a shed equipped with hot-water wash-out plant can run the same service with fewer engines than a shed only using ordinary methods of boiler washing.

Although each engineman takes the opportunity daily of checking the pressure at which the safety valves lift, they are also examined by a fitter each month, and a record kept. The gauges showing the level of the water in the boiler are examined, and the passages cleaned out each month. These passages, if choked with sediment, would cause a false reading of the water level.

An express locomotive has a high piston speed. The 6-feet 8-inch driving wheels revolve over four times each second when travelling at 60 mph. At this speed each piston, and its connecting rod, is averaging over 1,000 feet per minute, and as these and other moving parts change direction eight times each second, it will be realised that tremendous stresses are set up in all the moving parts. The failure of one might have serious consequence before the engine could be brought to rest by the driver.

In addition to the daily examination by the enginemen when preparing and stabling, and by the cleaners when cleaning these moving parts, the opportunity is taken each time a part is removed from the engine to examine it minutely for flaws. The tyres, to, must be examined for wear, and a record kept.

Formerly, cleaners had their own engines to follow up, and keep clean. This is not possible now with the more economical working of engines gained by double shifting. The cleaners, therefore, work in gangs. When cleaning they are gaining a knowledge of the engine, which will be to their advantage when promoted to fireman, and later to drivers. When they have attained a certain standard of knowledge, they are certified for firing if physically fit, and they usually commence on preparing and stabling work. On occasion they are called in emergency for firing on more important work, and being only human, are happier when on any work other than that of their own grade.

When an engine is stopped for a hot bearing, it is turned off into the stall, where the wheel drops are situated, and so placed that the wheels with the hot bearing are standing on the platform of the drops. The drops are worked by hydraulic power, and are like an ordinary station lift, or hoist, but there is a section of track across the platform.

After the wheels have been unfastened from the engine, the drop is lowered and it carries with it the wheels and brasses. When lowered, the wheels are rolled through a tunnel on to another hydraulic lift, where they are raised to ground level. The necessary repairs can then be conveniently carried out. This method is much cheaper than the old method of lifting the heavy engine, and rolling the wheels out from underneath. When the number of heating cases cannot all be dealt with on the drops, cranes, sometimes even the crane of the breakdown train is brought in to service ... [in such cases] the tender had to be un-coupled from the engine, but if ... dealt with on the drops, this would not ... be necessary.

Each shed has its tool vane for attending to breakdowns, or as our American cousins term it, the 'Wrecker'. At each of the large sheds there is a steam crane certified to lift up to 35 tons, and this is always ready at very short notice. The tool van gang are experienced men drawn from all grades of the shed staff. On receipt of a call they at once report to the foreman to arrange for their work to be carried on, and then proceed to the vans. The tool van consists of the large steam crane with runner [a trailer on which the jib rests] to carry the jib in its running position, a van carrying wood packing, another with an ample supply of tools for tackling jobs where the crane cannot be used, and lastly the vehicle in which the staff ride. In this coach there is a cooking range for providing hot meals, and, of course, a supply of food is carried.

Amongst the tools carried are hydraulic jacks for heavy lifts, block and wire rope tackle for very heavy pulls, and an oxy-acetylene cutting plant for cutting through any metal.

Out on the line each of the gang takes a pride in helping to clear the wreckage in record time.

After a big job, when gathered at the table in the riding van for their well-earned meal, tired out, none are too tired to compare their recent job with what they did at the same spot in 19–.

While not doubting their veracity, you must grant them the proverbial fisherman's licence for yarning.

The yard of a main line locomotive shed is one of the busiest areas of the line, for at a shed like York, it is a common matter for over 150 engines to enter, and also leave, the shed every twenty-four hours. This is at the rate of an engine either entering, or leaving, at less than five-minute intervals throughout the day.

Nearly all these engines clean their fires, and the ballast thus obtained, amounting to about 250 tons per week, has to be cleared away daily.

Railwaymen's Holidays

During the period we are dealing with, paid holidays had become a condition of service for most people, although for those working in industry, it was a condition that the works closed and everyone had to take their holiday at the same time. Clearly, this didn't happen on the actual railway or even in the running sheds, but the major railway workshops were a case apart and behaved like any other works or factory.

One advantage of working for the railway was concessionary travel, and the Swindon works holiday week required no less than thirty trains to accommodate the workers and their families. Not everyone travelled with the masses, however, and there would have been a few who would have either stayed at home or taken a regular train.

The Great Western Railway Magazine felt that the whole process of organising the trains deserved a page of photographs accompanied by a page-long report in 1933.

When the Great Western Railway company's Swindon works closes for the annual holiday it means that nearly half the population of the town of Swindon take advantage of this break and journey to holiday resorts in all parts of the British Isles. Swindonians are very catholic in their tastes and the majority confine their journeys to the Great Western; although Scotland, Wales, Ireland and the Channel Isles all have their adherents.

In great measure the wide variety of places chosen is due to the provision of special trains by the directors of the company to points on their own system, and the excellent 'fitting-in' of trains to make connections with cross-country services.

The origin of these special trains dates back to 1849, when the directors granted a 'special' for the conveyance of those of their members who were members of the 'Mechanics Institution'. About 500 members and their wives took part in that excursion. The concession of special trains for the holiday week has been continued ever since (except during the war period) and has grown until it is now necessary to run thirty trains to accommodate the works employees, their wives and families, numbering 26,800, whilst instead of only one destination there are upwards of 250.

Quite apart from the usual excitement attending holiday preparations there is a particular thrill belonging to this exodus from Swindon, and to those hundreds of thousands who, over the years, have travelled in these holiday trains, particularly the children, there is an intangible 'something' that is never wholly forgotten. Will they ever forget the hustle and bustle of the preceding night; getting up at 3.00am in the morning, in the ghostly light; finding their friends on the train and watching the sun rise through the windows of a railway compartment which is transformed into a golden chariot bearing them off to the sea?

Then again, to literally thousands, the holiday week has signalled 'wedding bells' on the preceding Thursday, so that advantage could be taken of the holiday and the special trains for the honeymoon.

No easy task confronts those who are responsible for the multitudinous arrangements to ensure that there shall be no hitch in transporting half the population of a town in seven hours. Preliminary arrangements are made several months beforehand, the venue chosen being ascertained from each employee, so that a general idea can be formed of the number who will take advantage of the special trains, and the places to which those trains will have to run. The complicated arrangements in connection with train timing, to avoid clashing with the ordinary passenger services and 'to fit in' the special trains to make connections with cross-country services, as may be necessary, all have to be gone into a long time before the holiday date; and the ordinary trains have to be strengthened to cover places to which there will not be a sufficient number of visitors to run special trains. Full details of the times of the trains on both the outward and return journeys are tabulated, together with the other necessary instructions, in order that everyone may be provided with tickets and a train time bill covering his own particular requirements.

All the coaches – about 415 – forming the trains, are assembled at Swindon in the various sidings and shunted into the positions from which the trains start, during the night (excepting for those trains starting from the station platforms), while engines to haul these long and heavy trains are also held in reserve until required.

Labelling the engines and trains is also a matter which has to be considered as, with so many trains all ready to receive their passengers, it is essential that the coaches should be fully and carefully labelled to their destinations.

Trains for Cornwall and North Wales were the first to leave, commencing with one for Penzance at 9.00pm on Thursday, July 12, while the last 'overnight' train was that for Newquay, at 12.20am. The first train to leave in the morning was that for Teignmouth, at 4.50am, and twenty-two other trains followed at short intervals until the last, which left for Barry Island at 8.05am.

Special services of the Swindon Corporation buses, as well as taxi-cabs and vehicles of every other description, were engaged in taking people from all parts of town to, fill the trains.

The places most favoured ... and the number travelling, are given below:

Weymouth	4,559	Paignton	783
Paddington	4,041	Blackpool	728
Weston-S.-M.	3,606	Exmouth	622
Barry Island	1,760	Newquay	593
St Ives	1,196	Tenby	582
Portsmouth	905	Penzance	539
Teignmouth	826	Jersey	463
North Wales	818		

Chapter 9

Setting Records

The period between the two world wars was one that saw the railways putting much emphasis on speed, with new records being set. This was despite the fact that for the first few years after grouping, the LNER and LMS were following an agreement that limited the shortest through-day journey between London and either Edinburgh or Glasgow to eight and a half hours, so that sleepers were actually faster than the day trains. This nonsense was adhered to so thoroughly that when a non-stop service was introduced between King's Cross and Edinburgh Waverley, the train actually became slower and a following train making four stops took the same time. This ridiculous situation was a throw-back to the inter-company, or inter-groups of companies, races of the 1890s, which were taken to a dangerous extreme, but locomotives had improved by the early 1920s and end-to-end journey times of six and a half hours or less were not only achievable, but safely so.

There were, of course, two distinct types of record. There was the absolute speed record achieved most notably by the LNER's locomotive No. 4468 *Mallard*, and then there were the *fastest services*, a distinction held by the LNER at the time of grouping, but which passed to the GWR with the train that was known as the 'Cheltenham Flyer', albeit the title was unofficial. This was a world record for a while; Canadian Pacific and then later the *Deutschebahn* held it.

None of the accounts available were by serving engine drivers or guards, which is a shame, but it is also the case that the world record for steam, still unbeaten, set by the famous LNER Pacific locomotive No. 4468 *Mallard* was such a spur-of-the-moment event that even the company's own magazine had to reprint an account from the *Railway Gazette*.

King's Cross to Newcastle

Given the agreement between the East and West Coast companies, the LNER initially concentrated its efforts on the run between London and Newcastle. When introduced on 11 July 1927, this was the longest non-stop railway service in the world, with the train completing the 268 miles in five and a half hours, which was less than 50 mph on average. Five A1 Pacific locomotives provided the stud for this service, with three based at King's Cross and two at Gateshead. The train was an advance portion of the 'Flying Scotsman' express, although the famous locomotive of that name was not one of the stud, thus relieving pressure on the main train at peak periods. The non-stop train ran only on summer Mondays, Thursdays, Fridays and Saturdays; the busiest days of the week.

The inaugural run was covered by the *London & North Eastern Railway Magazine*.

To Driver A. Pibworth and Fireman H. Mutton fell the honour of making the initial run with the [No. 4475] *Flying Fox* engine. Driver T. Blades and Fireman W. Morris, Gateshead, accomplished the second. There was a good send-off from King's Cross, and at many places en route, notably at York, big crowds assembled and cheered enthusiastically the *Flying Fox*'s progress. Newcastle was reached at the precise scheduled time (3.20pm), and when the train drew up on No. 8 platform there was a dense and enthusiastic crowd awaiting it. The Lord Mayor of Newcastle (Mr Arthur W. Lambert) and the Sheriff (Mr R. Stanley Dalgliesh) gave the train crew an official welcome, and there were also present many prominent businessmen and North Eastern Area railway officers … The engine crew seemed quite taken by surprise at the warmth of their welcome. Immediately the driver and fireman descended from the footplate telegraph messages were thrust into their hands from the Chief General Manager congratulating them on their successful run. The Lord Mayor then handed to the men briar pipes as a souvenir from the Divisional General Manager, Mr George Davidson.

The second run was made on Thursday, July 14, by Driver T. Blades and Fireman W. Morrris, both of Gateshead, with engine [No. 2569] *Gladiateur* [sic]. On this occasion also the run was very successful, the train arriving at Newcastle six minutes ahead of schedule. Souvenir pipes were handed to the driver and fireman by Mr Stedman, assistant locomotive running superintendent.

The first run prompted a passenger on the train, who simply identified himself as 'J.E.L.', to send the LNER a few verses on the achievement:

'Old Pibs' he was a railwayman
For engine craft renowned,
He drove the non-stop Flying Fox
Up to Newcastle Town.

The crowd upon the platform cheer,
The signal arms are down,
And Flying Fox is set to win
This record run from Town.

Away from London on the 'dot',
They sped along the main
The spirit of 'George Stephenson'
Was surely with that train.

As they sped, and on past York
And on past Durham too,
They never stopped when they set out
Until they had got through.

And there upon the platform stood
The Mayor in chain and gown
To welcome 'Pib's and both his 'pals'
Up to Newcastle Town.

We passengers behind the Fox
Appreciate this run,
And like the General Manager,
We say to 'Pibs' 'Well Done'.

The Non-Stop 'Flying Scotsman'

This was a real achievement. The excitement shown by the crowds remind us that at the time railways were *the* advanced technology of the day, and in particular the steam engine, even though many were hard at work on the diesel and the electric as alternative forms of propulsion. The LNER even at one time experimented with a hybrid 'steam-diesel' in an attempt to make the best of both forms of propulsion. So, even while the Southern Railway was showing the way with electric multiple unit working, and German railways were setting the first diesel records, steam showed no sign of being in decline.

The following year, on 1 May 1928, the 'Flying Scotsman' took the crown as the world's longest non-stop railway service. This, naturally enough, attracted still more attention, with a through journey of 392.7 miles between King's Cross and Edinburgh Waverley.

The down departure from King's Cross was preceded by an inspection of the locomotive and train by the Lord Mayor of London, even though the station was outside the City of London, and Sir Ralph Wedgewood, the LNER's Chief General Manager. In the opposite direction, the balancing working from Waverley was 'officially recognised' by Bailie Hay and his daughter, with the drivers and firemen [two of each for this marathon journey] presented with rosettes of black and white, the colours of the city of Edinburgh, and also silver badges depicting the city's coat of arms. The driver taking the first turn was presented with a horse shoe adorned with black and white streamers.

The *London & North Eastern Railway Magazine* once again covered the journey, which on this occasion also included an account by a 'Looker On' and 'A Locomotive Inspector's Impressions' by one A. Renton, but this time there was no poetry.

Renton's impressions first.

The first of May, 1928, is a day that will stand for many years in the memory of LNER employees, and especially those connected with the depots from which the great machines set out for their first non-stop run between Edinburgh Waverley and London King's Cross, and vice versa.

To ensure success on the initial run, no little care and forethought was required, and I was early at Haymarket locomotive sheds to see that no hitch occurred in the final preparation of 'Super-Pacific' engine No. 2580 *Shotover* for its 392 miles journey to King's Cross. After the engine had been properly oiled and examined, it was run light to Waverley, where it was attached by means of a buck-eye coupling to the train, which consisted of eleven vehicles (232 tons). The corridor provided in the tender for the locomotive men changing over on the journey was an innovation that proved most attractive, and many had the privilege of being shown through before the train started.

At 10.00am prompt, the engine started out of the station to the accompaniment of cheering and expressions of goodwill. We were off; the wheels were in motion, and we trusted that nothing would occur to stop their motion until King's Cross station was reached. A heavy Scotch mist, so dense that at some points fog signalmen were on duty, failed to damp our spirits in any way. Running very steadily, Berwick was passed at booked time, and the tank was replenished at Lucker troughs, while running, by means of the pick-up scoop, to carry us to Danby Wiske, a distance of ninety-nine miles, where a further supply of water was similarly obtained. Everything was found to be running very smoothly. Newcastle was passed three minutes late, due to engineer's slows, Darlington at time, York and Doncaster two minutes ahead, Grantham and Peterborough one minute ahead, Hitchin two minutes late due to slow, and King's Cross was reached one minute ahead of time, the train arriving at No. 1 platform at 6.14pm, the wheels coming to rest then for the first time since leaving Edinburgh.

At Tollerton, the Edinburgh Haymarket driver and fireman were relieved by the King's Cross men who travelled from Edinburgh in a reserved compartment of the train, and now passed to the engine via the corridor in the tender; the Edinburgh men passing through to the train and resting for the remainder of the journey.

At principal stations en route there was lusty cheering from gatherings impressed with the importance of the occasion, the locomotive centres being particularly enthusiastic. On arrival at King's Cross the reception was really great, the platform from end to end being crowded with spectators vying with each other in the warmth of their welcome. Mr Whitelaw, the Chairman, was there to welcome us on arrival, and he presented the drivers and firemen with beautiful pocket books, each bearing a suitable inscription to mark the occasion, and no doubt these mementoes will be treasured by the recipients and be retained as heirlooms long after we older folk have ceased to worry about non-stop runs.

The feat is a great compliment to Mr Gresley, the Chief Mechanical Engineer. The performance of the engine was splendid in every respect, and in the opinion of the enginemen and myself, nothing finer in the shape of a steam locomotive could be asked for. The engine covered 392 miles, with a train load equal to 323 tons, on a coal consumption including lighting and raising steam, of 6 tons, 34.02-lb of coal consumed per engine-mile, and a water consumption that averaged about 2,500 gallons per 100 miles. Full steam pressure was maintained throughout, the engine still steaming freely during the latter part of the journey, whilst the bearing showed no sign of heat on the completion of the journey.

Naturally, I am proud of having been associated with the engine men on this first non-stop run on our line between Edinburgh and London, and as it was a great achievement, I consider it 'something to write home about.'

An achievement, but look at the wasted opportunity with a through journey time of eight and a half hours without stops or checks. Within a decade, the through time would be down to a more exciting and business-like six hours.

Nevertheless, nothing else was faster, and the days of intensive internal commercial air services were some way ahead, although the railways, with the exception of the LNER, were amongst the pioneers of air travel within the British Isles.

The other eye-witness was 'Looker On'.

'May-Day' 1928, will long be remembered on the LNER. It was a great day – a day of realisation, enthusiasm and triumph, all along the East Coast route. For weeks there had been extra activity of a sectional and subdued sort amongst train operators, engine and carriage folk, track and lever men, and many other experts; preparing, planning and plotting.

Hairdressers, water-trough workers, blue print enthusiasts and those who deal with lubricated bearings and motion parts, exerted themselves for a united effort – the running of a new 'Flying Scotsman', King's Cross and Edinburgh, without stop, 392 miles – as the orange and green posters on the hoardings put it.

Then at last as the day dawned, there were white topped carriages in King's Cross and Waverley with white-coated hairdressers as colleagues for the chefs and lady attendant in neat brown uniforms, reserved seats men, newsmen and guards.

And 'Pacific' locomotives – engines known to thousands of enthusiasts, but with corridor tenders and double crews. Drivers Pibworth and Blades, with Firemen Goddard and Morris found a foothold on No. 4472 whilst at Waverley, Drivers Henderson and Day, with Firemen MacKenzie and Gray, aboard No. 2580.

It wanted but a few minutes to ten when the Lord Mayor of London with the Chief, and Bailie Hay with Miss Hay and Mr Calder, appeared on the respective platforms crowded to capacity with all manner of folk. 'First stop Edinburgh' and 'First stop London' rang out, the guards' whistles shrilled and mighty cheers went up the station roofs as the two trains started.

All along the line there were knots, groups and crowds wellwishers watching the passing of the non-stop trains. Through Peterborough and Grantham, through Berwick and Newcastle, they roared, whilst Mr George Davidson and the York contingent got a good view as the two trains thundered through at lunch time. But they could hardly hear the long and loud shrieks of salute from the two engine whistles which sounded across the fields near Alne and blended into a single note of triumph marking the halfway line of the first runs.

Daylight was dimming when their destinations were reached – the two trains (the 'up' and the 'down') steaming into their stations towards more crowds and cheers.

'Congratulations to the LNER'. 'A wonderful achievement performed without the slightest hitch,' 'A new public service,' 'A British Railway Triumph,' 'A fine start,' 'Records made and broken' – so the press had it and for once they were right, thanks to clever team work on the part of all concerned.

But there was more to come.

The World's Fastest Train Run

So ran the headline in *The Great Western Railway Magazine* with an account of the accelerated 'Cheltenham Flyer' when this was introduced on 14 September 1931. As the report shows, the title had already been lost once. One problem was, of course, that the train really only set records between Swindon and Paddington, while between Cheltenham and Swindon its speed was little better than any other train. This account was penned by 'W.G.C.'

The world's fastest train-run in daily service has been restored to Britain by the Great Western Railway company. A feature of the company's winter train service which came into operation on Monday, September 14, was an acceleration of certain expresses. In pride of position among these was the 2.30pm train from Cheltenham, popularly known as the 'Cheltenham Flyer'. It has been given the world's record timing over the seventy-seven and a quarter miles from Swindon, where it makes its last call, *en route* to Paddington. Its average speed, from start to stop, is 69.2 miles per hour. Previously, since July 1929, this train was timed to leave Swindon at 3.45pm and to arrive at Paddington at 4.55pm, giving an average speed of 66.2 miles per hour. Until April last, this was the fastest regularly scheduled start-to-stop run in the world. Then the Canadian Pacific Railway introduced a train-timing over the 124 miles between Montreal and Smith's Falls, at an average speed of 68.9 miles per hour. Now, however, the 'Cheltenham Flyer' is scheduled to leave Swindon at 3.48pm (three minutes later) and to arrive at Paddington the same time as before. On the day that the new timing came into operation, the train made a remarkable run, which must remain a notable performance among many wonderful Great Western train-speed achievements.

Great public interest was taken in the inaugural run, and when the train arrived at Swindon at 3.44pm, hauled by engine No. 5000, *Launceston Castle*, there was a large company of well-wishers present, including railway officials, journalists, press photographers and railway enthusiasts. Mr C.B. Collett, the Chief Mechanical Engineer of the Great Western Railway, was there, with his assistant, Mr W.A. Stanier. Inspector H.J. Robinson was on the footplate with Driver J.W. Street and Fireman F.W. Shearer, as was also Mr John Haygate, who was that evening broadcasting an account of the run for the British Broadcasting Company.

The load behind the tender consisted of six coaches, including a tea car. There were a good number of passengers aboard when the train arrived at Swindon, where many more joined it, including the writer.

Precisely at 3.48pm the 'right-away' was given, and the train started on its run. As soon as we were free of the station, speed began appreciably to accelerate. At Shrivenham we were getting well under way, and soon after we were doing a mile a minute, whilst at Uffington the speed was in the neighbourhood of 80 miles per hour. The pace did not drop below 80 until we were within a couple of miles or so of Paddington.

It was evident that the news had spread along the line that something exceptional was being undertaken in the way of speeds, for harvesters in the fields and others stopped their work to see the 'Flyer' pass and to cheer her on her way. This was particularly the case when passing the RAF and RAOD [Royal Army Ordnance Depot] depots at Didcot, where large numbers congregated along the line, whilst from the lofty roof of the Great Western Railway forage store at Didcot, a small party waved encouragement as we flashed by.

Hereabouts, speed increased, and a good 84 miles per hour was maintained through Cholsey and Moulsford, Goring, Pangbourne, and Tilehurst. At Reading, passed at approximately 4.20pm, speed had increased to around 85 miles per hour.

Throughout the trip the pace was much more real than apparent. We were certainly speeding, but there was no sense of very high speed. Passengers passed to and from the tea car and took their meal in perfect comfort. There was an entire absence of jolting or oscillation.

A large crowd had congregated at Reading to see the 'Flyer' pass. From this point onward there was further steady acceleration as we passed Twyford and Maidenhead. At Taplow we were doing our best speed so far, which was around about 86 miles per hour. This was well maintained for a considerable distance.

On we flew, through Slough, where we saw the sun for the first time. Here employees on the vast trading estates turned out in good numbers to see us flash past. The road over bridge near the station was black with spectators. Soon we were through Langley, Iver, West Drayton and Hayes. At all these places people had turned out to give us a hearty wave, but perhaps the largest concourse of sightseers were those who packed the road bridge at Southall, which we passed at a speed somewhere approaching 86½ miles per hour.

At all the factories along this length of line workers were assembled. Hanwell, the Ealings and Acton were all passed without any slackening of this speed. It was after passing Westbourne Park that we felt the gradual application of the brakes, and were going quite quietly at Royal Oak. We glided into Paddington station with the hands of the big clock just short of the 4.48 indication, having done the trip start-to-stop not at the scheduled world record speed of 69.2 miles an hour, but in a portion of a minute under the hour! We had actually knocked a full seven minutes out of the new accelerated schedule.

Then followed a great rush of admirers to the footplate, and the station rang with cheer on cheer for the engine crew. A bouquet of flowers was handed to the driver, whilst passengers and others almost fought for the privilege of grasping the hands of the trustworthy engineman who had brought us up at record speed, made railway history, and added yet another to the many speed triumphs of the Great Western Railway.

The feature of the trip was not the accomplishment of any abnormally high speed, so much as the consistent running over sixty-odd miles at speeds over 80 miles per hour. The average speed for the whole run was 77.9 miles per hour, and the official time taken, 59½ minutes. The highest bursts of speed were those between Slough and Southall, when 86.6 miles per hour was attained, and between Didcot and Reading, when the average was 85 miles an hour.

On the second day of its new timing, the 'Cheltenham Flyer' actually surpassed its previous day's performance. On this occasion, the load was seven vehicles (219 tons) … the journey was accomplished in fifty-eight minutes, the average speed being 79.9 miles per hour.

Nevertheless, a later issue of the magazine included an account by the engine driver, Mr J.W. Street, of a flight in a light aircraft over the train. When the event was organised the Master of Semphill and Street was allowed to take his wife with him, marking the occasion of their first flight. The Master of Semphill preceded this little treat with a 'speed kings' lunch, with the other guests including the world air-speed record holder, Flight-Lieutenant Stainforth; Sir Malcolm Campbell, the world land- speed record holder; J.S. Wright, the motor-cycle record holder, and others, including Amy Johnson, the aviatrix.

Unfortunately he says little about the aircraft other than that it was a closed-cabin monoplane, with two passengers sitting behind the pilot, Captain Max Findlay. Perhaps it was a de Havilland Puss Moth. The account tells us much about the relative performance of the light aircraft of the day.

> Thinking that we were not flying at a very great speed I asked Captain Findlay what it was, and to my great surprise he said 80 mph, but that there was a head-wind velocity of 35 mph ... We flew much lower when nearing Swindon, but not any slower ... I instantly recognised the train and informed Captain Findlay, who turned the plane on its side, swooped down and encircled the train. This he did time and time again. The reason for our flying in this way was that our cruising speed, as I have mentioned, was 95 mph (sic), and the wind (now blowing with the train) had a velocity of 35 mph, thus preventing us from flying alongside the train for any distance ... We lost sight of the 'Flyer' when she passed through the cuttings at Pangbourne and Tilehurst ...

A rare treat for an engine driver at a time when few people had flown.

The Immortal *Mallard*

The *London & North Eastern Railway Magazine* had to rely on the *Railway Gazette* for a first-hand account of the record of 126 mph set by the A4 Pacific locomotive No. 4468 *Mallard* on Sunday 3 July 1938. The record stands to this day for steam locomotives, and is remarkable not just for that but because she had worn valves and was driven by a driver known for thrashing his engines.

On Sunday 3 July 1938, during a series of high-speed brake trials on the main line between Peterborough and Grantham, the opportunity was taken to make an attempt on the world speed record for railways using the A4 locomotive No. 4468 *Mallard*. Although the load was far less than a full train, it was no light weight either, with three twin articulated carriages from the spare 'Coronation' set and the company's dynamometer car, making seven vehicles in all with an empty weight of 236.5 tons, or 240 tons with officials and equipment aboard. *Mallard* was chosen because she was one of three A4 locomotives to have the Kylchap exhaust arrangements, which included a double blast-pipe and chimney. The decision to find out how fast the locomotive could run with the seven vehicle load seems to have been almost a spur of the moment decision.

Mallard took her rake of carriages through Grantham station at just 24 mph because of permanent way work, and then accelerated to almost 60 mph over the next two and a half miles, up a rising gradient of 1 in 200, eventually reaching almost 75 mph over the next mile-and-a-half to Stoke summit, again over a further stretch at 1 in 200. Descending Stoke Bank, the speed rose to 116 mph, and then to 119 mph, and then crossed the 120 mph mark where it stayed for the next three miles, reaching a maximum of 126 mph. The locomotive maintained a speed of between 123 mph and 126 mph for nearly two miles. The record-breaking run was then curtailed as the opportunity was taken to conduct a brake test from such a high speed and the train was approaching the curve at Essendine, which also included several sets of points, and it was thought unwise to take these at such a high speed.

As *The Railway Gazette* put it:

> ... the speed was over 120 mph for about three miles, and as the boiler was finding steam steadily for the heavy demand created by 40 per cent cut-off, with full regulator, there seems no reason why this speed should not have been continued down the 1 in 264 beyond Essendine. In any event, the record shows the maximum to have been no merely momentary peak, but maintained at an even figure for a greater distance than any of the previous records, apart from the forty-three miles continuously at 100 mph average of *Silver Link* in the 'Silver Jubilee' trail of September 27, 1935 ...

This was a greater achievement than generally realised, not just because it has never been beaten anywhere, but because far from being specially prepared, *Mallard* had worn valves and was driven hard by a driver, J. Duddington, of Doncaster, known for thrashing his loco-motives. Had she been properly prepared and all valve clearances correct, the record might have been set even higher. As it was, those on the footplate could smell the machinery as it overheated and the locomotive needed major workshop attention afterwards.

Many claim that locomotives of the day operating in the United States and Germany could have matched or even exceeded this record, but the point is that they didn't. One would have expected the

L M S SPECIALS—THE WORKS OUTING

One indication of how things have changed is that, even in a period of growing competition from road transport, the railways could still provide special trains at cheap fares for the annual works outing, although the service was clearly not appreciated by this commercial traveller. (*LMS*)

PORTER (to commercial traveller, who has arrived unexpectedly):—" Ain't it funny, sir, as 'ow we've taken *them* away cheap, and brought *you* here for nothing ? "

This is *Tangmere* as Ransome-Wallis would have found her, un-rebuilt, with a train of mixed Bulleid and Maunsell rolling stock. (*HMRS AEV902*)

Dr Syn still runs on the Romney, Hythe & Dymchurch Railway, and while the locomotive on her own looks large, the driver with head and shoulders above the cab gives the game away. *(RH&DR)*

Typical of the railway scene on the Isle of Wight, where A.B. Macleod honed his management skills, is this O2-class locomotive, *Brading*, on the pier at Ryde. *(HMRS AEP312)*

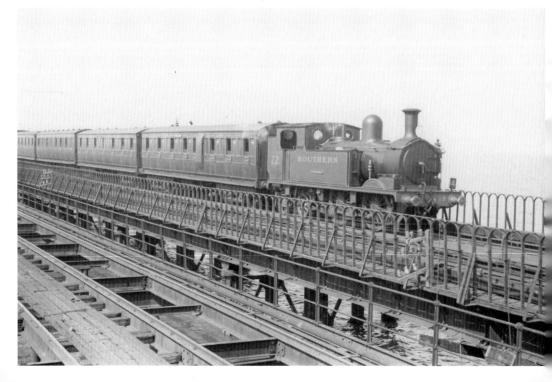

Locomotive sheds were dirty places, even on the Great Western. This is *King Edward VI* at the coaling stage in 1930. This was an old-fashioned way of coaling even at that time as many railways used coaling towers. (*HMRS ABX120*)

A coaling tower typical of the many introduced between the two world wars in an attempt to improve productivity. This type was known as a 'Cenotaph' and was at Cambridge on the LNER. (*HMRS AER 132*)

A locomotive 'running light', that is without carriages or wagons, leaves a tunnel. One of the filthiest jobs on the steam railway was checking tunnel linings. (*HMRS ADM 604*)

The immortal *Mallard* whose record of 126 mph for a steam locomotive remains unbeaten.

Not as fast as *Mallard*, but a daily commercial service, this is the 'Cheltenham Spa Express' leaving Paddington, but the train was more usually known to the public as the 'Cheltenham Flyer'. (*HMRS AAA822*)

Almost too close for comfort. An ex-Midland Railway 4-4-0 runs slowly past men working on the track in 1930. (*HMRS AEW 220*)

Breakdown cranes were positioned at strategic points across the railway system ready for breakdowns or accidents and derailments, but could also be used to help with civil engineering work. (*HMRS AEU 832*)

Despite the pressure to electrify, and the progress made by the Southern Railway which had the world's largest suburban electric system, many still felt that steam provided the best means of traction, and tank engines like this were worked very hard indeed. (*HMRS AAB 112*)

Not all of the fastest steam locomotives were streamlined. This is an LMS Princess Royal-class locomotive with the 'Mid-Day Scot' before streamlining became fashionable. (*HMRS AEU 205*)

From the earliest days of the railways, the mail was an important traffic and was carried in special travelling post office carriages such as this, with the mail dropped off and picked up at speed while sorters worked through the night aboard the train. This was an LMS travelling post office. (*HMRS AAJ 315*)

A brief interlude in the busy signal box at Settle Junction on the former Midland Railway line between St Pancras and Glasgow. (*HMRS ACW805*)

"I'M READY"

TAKE YOUR DOG
WITH YOU BY RAIL

Return Tickets at Single Rate

DRINKING WATER FOR DOGS CAN BE OBTAINED FROM STATION REFRESHMENT
ROOMS, OR ON REQUEST TO A MEMBER OF THE STATION STAFF.

G.W.R.   LMS   L·N·E·R   S.R.

Passengers were encouraged to take their dogs with them, with drinking water available on request at stations.

Germans, whose dictator had a thirst for propaganda, to have set a new record if they had been able. Others have also suggested that the LMS Duchess-class could have matched or exceeded the record, but again, this did not happen. It might be pertinent to note that while the LNER cut the London to Edinburgh journey time of the 'Flying Scotsman' to just six hours, the rival LMS service to Glasgow took thirty minutes longer.

Chapter 10

On the Track

The standard of railway track varied between companies, although both the GWR and the LMS made much of the quality of their lines, well ballasted and well laid. The Southern inherited some poor track and bad ballast from its predecessors, and especially the London Chatham & Dover and South Eastern Railways. Obviously, the best track was reserved for those lines carrying the fast expresses, while minor branch lines and sidings had the poorest. Track could be turned so that one the 'inside' was worn, it could be switched around and the former 'outside' turned inside. Track was also cascaded, as track too worn for high speed running could be used on branches or in sidings.

While work was generally much filthier, the lack of retention toilets meant that working on the track could be especially unpleasant, especially in hot weather, and not all of this material hit the track, much of it also struck the underside and axles of rolling stock.

Our first account of being down on the track relates to a crossing of the Forth Bridge, and is strictly not a working account at all, but then the accounts of riding on the footplate could hardly be classified as working accounts; and like the following have been included because of the light they throw on the steam railway.

Across the Forth

The *London & North Eastern Railway Magazine* clearly decided that its readers should know more about the great bridge across the Forth, completed in 1890. Although worked by the North British Railway once opened, this company had been so impoverished by the Tay Bridge disaster some years earlier that it could only bridge the Forth with the collaboration and investment of the Midland Railway (which passed into the LMS in 1923), the Great Northern and North Eastern Railways.

This is a massive and even monumental structure, which has been considered for World Heritage status, although that might be a mixed blessing as it is still very much part of a working railway and carries passenger and freight trains, with the latter in recent years having been as heavy as 1,700 tons.

Unusually, this account was written jointly by J.L. Hunt and S.W. Ellis.

Many readers have doubtless crossed the Firth of Forth via the magnificent bridge whose 51,000 tons of steel bear the burden of scores of trains each day. To walk, instead of ride, however, is quite an adventure and an experience well worth the relating.

Leaving a northbound train at Dalmeny, we first called at the offices of the Forth Bridge Railway Company (by whose kind permission the facility was arranged) [A statutory company created for the bridge, this was owned by the four railway companies mentioned above, although by this time it had the LNER as the major shareholder and the LMS as the junior partner.], and here had our authority countersigned and officially stamped. Thus armed we commenced the trip, leaving the permit at the watchman's hut, where we signed the register and received useful advice.

Once on the approach, we were 'all eyes', determined not to overlook any point of interest, and this quarter-mile was soon traversed, affording as it certainly does a wonderful view not only of the Firth, but of the bridge, from an unusual angle. However, we had by now arrived at the massive pillars which form the entrance to the main steelwork, and were gazing in open-mouthed amazement at the maze of girders and tubular supports.

The thrill of actually walking in this marvellous avenue is indescribable, our progress being but slow as we investigated each section of this engineering triumph. Had we not been counselled to look for the golden rivet placed in position by King George V (then Prince of Wales) in 1890, it is certain that we should have missed it amongst the 5,000,000 fellow rivets, so enthralled were we by the endless marvels before our eyes.

In all, seven trains passed over the bridge during our walk, five of them on 'our' side, causing us to cling to the rail for comfort of support more than the actual need of it, there being heaps of room. One striking feature as the trains approached was the complete disappearance of the men working on the permanent way, and we found that they were able to leave by means of manholes leading to ladders under the structure, and upon which the men stand until the trains have passed. Another equally striking point was the exceptionally cordial greetings voiced by these men, who keep a smiling face whilst performing duties which, to the layman, appear extremely dangerous. Apart from the 5,000 men who were employed day and night for seven years in the building of the bridge, there is this permanent staff always at work painting and repairing their masterpiece, recommencing operations at one end immediately they have finished at the other.

Although the main spans comprise two of 1,710 feet and another two of 680 feet, it was difficult to realise which of these we were in during our crossing, the sky being the only real guide as to the respective height of the spans. Walking on the 'up', or south side, we had an unforgettable sight of the distant North Sea, with the cargo and pleasure steamers constantly passing to and from the neighbouring port of Rosyth. Another point of interest was the 'Island', which provides residence for the workmen and stores for their materials, in addition to giving much of the support for the main foundations, the work of which starts 91 feet below water level and reaches its highest peak 360 feet above the Forth.

The complete distance of one mile and a half was completed in just over an hour, and as we left our path at North Queensferry station, we were able to say with all sincerity it had been an hour of crowded life, each second of which had given the greatest pleasure, in fact, 'enjoyable education'.

For those living nearby, the endurance of the bridge is often compared with that of the much newer road bridge, opened in 1960, which is suffering corrosion to its suspension cables. Victorian over-engineering and the strength of a cantilever bridge may be decried, but the railway bridge has survived. A sign of the times, however, is that a new bridge is being built that will offer no greater provision than the existing road bridge, so it is to be hoped that the current road bridge will remain open at least for lighter vehicles.

The Platelayer

Fundamental to the safety and reliability of the railway was, and remains, the platelayer, and in the days of steam and even through to early electric and diesel days, he also had other duties to perform in fog. It seems that this is more of a descriptive piece about the duties of a platelayer than a first-hand personal account, although the author of the piece, one H.E. Saunders, does not have any job title in his by-line in the *LMS Magazine*.

The company spent £4.5 million in 1927 on track maintenance, of which £3 million was accounted for by wages.

> ... The platelayer is a railway servant whom the travelling public rarely see actually at work. When trains are passing along the line, platelayers can often be observed standing idle by the line side, leaning on their shovels or in some other easy attitude. This is, of course, because they must stand clear when trains are passing. The platelayer is not provided with uniform clothing to attract people's attention, and therefore he is probably overlooked by the travelling public, although his services are actually of the greatest value ... The permanent way is the foundation of every railway, and the platelayers' duty is to look after its upkeep. How successfully our men do this is proved by the smooth, easy, and comfortable travelling which fully justifies the LMS claim to have 'The Best Permanent Way in the World'.
>
> The platelayer is required to be an 'A1' man from the medical point of view, and before engagement is required to pass a stringent test, particularly as regards eyesight and colour vision. He is also required to be of powerful physique, so that he may do his share in manipulating the 60-feet railway metals, which weigh more than three-quarters of a ton each. The chairs which support the rails also weigh 46-lb each, and the timber sleeper to which the chairs are attached weighs about 1¼ cwts [140 lb]. From these particulars it will be seen how necessary it is to have strong, active men as platelayers. It is also necessary for him to be an intelligent man, as he is required to be familiar with and act promptly in accordance with the instructions laid down for his guidance in the Book of Rules and Regulations. In case of mishap, he is subject to emergency calls which must be responded to promptly, even if he is off duty. These calls are fairly frequent in heavily worked places, where vehicles are sometimes derailed during shunting; but they rarely occur away from busy centres. Fortunately, calls consequent upon accidents to passenger trains are extremely rare.

Platelayers when on the line are called upon to exercise great vigilance to keep out of the way of moving vehicles, and special look-out men are provided for their protection in many cases.

When fog descends upon us, the platelayer is at once called upon, whether by day or night, to take up duty at the signal post for which he is rostered, there to act instead of the lighted signal which, owing to the fog, cannot be seen by drivers of approaching trains. He is provided with a hand lamp and flags to show white, red and green signals, and a supply of detonators.

When the fixed signal is at danger, his duty is to place on the line one of the detonators which, when exploded by being run over, warns the driver that the line is not clear. These detonators, if not run over and exploded, are, upon the lowering of the signal removed or knocked off by the fogman. 'Fogging'. As one can imagine, is not a pleasant duty, but the fogman is made as comfortable as circumstances will permit, being supplied with a brazier fire and a warm overcoat, He is also visited at his post at intervals.

Generally speaking, each platelayer has to look after the maintenance of about one mile of permanent way. It has been found most suitable and economical to form small gangs consisting of four or five men for this purpose, the four-man gangs caring for about four miles of track, and the five-man gangs for about five miles of single line.

Platelayers' duties are numerous. First of all, early each morning, the length of line is looked over and examined from end to end to see that all is in order, and loose keys, bolts or screws are tightened or replaced, points carefully examined, oiled and cleaned (if necessary adjusted), and in frosty weather especially attended to so that they may be kept free from snow and ice. The crossings and line itself are kept to gauge and repaired, lifted or slewed as may be necessary to retain line and level, so that good running may be secured, and any defective material is replaced. All this work has of necessity to be performed between the passage of trains. So that sheep and other animals may not get on to the line, fences have to be kept in an efficient state. If the fences are of the hedge description, they are dug around and trimmed periodically. Bridges both under and over the railway are carefully examined. In extremely wet weather, special attention is paid to the railway banks or cuttings to watch for landslips, and watercourses, culverts, &c., also specially attended to in order to prevent flooding. To assist drainage, side ditches and drains are kept clear, and no weeds or grass are allowed to grow in the ballast. The line generally is kept clear of rubbish which has a habit of accumulating from day to day, any articles found lying on the line (and it is rather strange how some descriptions of articles come to get on the line) being picked up and taken to the nearest station. The grass on slops is in season mown and generally burnt, but sometimes in country districts in country districts where grass is of good quality it is sold to neighbouring farmers to make hay.

The top ballasting of the permanent way on main lines is now generally composed of broken stone or other description of heavy material, such as slag from iron foundries, &c. This has been found to provide the best drainage, and proves less dusty than coal, cinders or ashes, which was formerly the material employed as 'ballast'. Broken stone ballast is also practically everlasting, and does not require renewal as in the case of ballast composed of ashes, which after a time becomes waterlogged, or 'spent', besides which it can be hand-screened by the platelayers in the course of their ordinary duties to abstract fine dust thrown out through the chimneys of locomotives, soot and other dirty material. The extracted rubbish is then cast away and each screening of stone ballast thrown back onto the line.

In the summer, especially if the weather is hot, each rail is examined to see that proper spaces exist between the rail ends to allow for expansion, as otherwise there is the possibility of the permanent way being forced out of line, which might cause a serious accident. The plates which fasten one rail to the next and the bolts to same are cleaned and oiled once a year to assist expansion or contraction, and to prevent the bolts themselves becoming corroded ... but these are not all his duties, as, in addition, he is called upon to unload coal, sand &c., for stations, signal boxes &c., and performs other laborious work from time to time, He also has a considerable amount of week-end and Sunday duty, especially with points and crossings at heavily-worked places where the crossings are soon worn out and require replacement. This work can only be accomplished when traffic is lightest, as to do it at other times would mean disorganising the train services. There are places known on our line where new 95-lb per yard crossings have become worn out for main line use in six weeks ... At other places they will wear as many years or more.

The ordinary maintenance platelayer does not carry out the actual renewal of his permanent way when the time arrives for this. This renewal, or 'relaying', as it is called, is usually performed by large gangs of men who travel about from place to place for this special purpose.

The Editor as Platelayer

While one editor of the *Great Western Railway Magazine* favoured acting as an observer, riding in a travelling post office or being at Paddington whilst the newspaper trains were loaded in the middle of the night, another, Edward Hadley, favoured trying the various jobs himself. Usually, he wrote his pieces in the third person, but on this occasion, the first person was used. A word of warning: this was written in the days before political correctness.

A unique experience has been mine. For a week last month I worked as an 'underman' in a gang of platelayers.

In connection with accident prevention work, I intended to write a book for platelayers, dealing with the risks of injury in their occupation, and describing the best means of securing safety at their work. It was manifest that for this task nothing could be more helpful to me than practical experience. Therefore, I sought an opportunity of 'going through the mill', and made my idea known to the company's chief engineer.

'Do you want *to see* the work of the platelayer, or actually to be a platelayer and *to do* the work yourself?' he asked.

'I want really to be a platelayer for a week,' said I.

'And where do you wish to work – on the main line, or on a branch line where it would be safer?'

I explained that my purpose was to see and to know the actual risks and dangers of a platelayer's job, and for this reason the place where these would be 'thickest' would suit me best.

The chief engineer reflected for a while, and then with fatherly solicitude – which I greatly appreciate, advised me first of all to make sure that my heart was sound and my general bodily condition equal to the strain the work would involve. Subject to the certification of my physical fitness, he would arrange for me to be employed as an 'underman' in a main line gang in the London division.

Then I went to the doctor. His certificate was satisfactory, and I was handed over to the London divisional engineer, Mr R.C. Kirkpatrick, who placed me in the hands of the divisional inspector, Mr E. Ginger, with the emphatic but kindly warning, 'Be extremely careful and vigilant; keep your wits about you every moment. We don't want to lose you.'

Mr Ginger was splendid. He entered into the spirit of the thing, and not only attached me to the most suitable gang, but arranged with the ganger for the week's work to be varied, so as to comprise practically every kind of job that platelayers have to do.

I was to start on Monday. On the previous Saturday, at noon, Mr Ginger took me to the platelayer's cabin – of No. 4 Gang – to make the acquaintance of the ganger and my prospective mates.

In the fraternity of platelayers, surnames are dropped. I was introduced as 'Dick', and the ganger (E. Gerrard) as 'Ted'. Then there were 'Old Jim; and 'Young Jim', 'Joe' (a native of the West Indies), another 'Joe', Sam, George, and 'Jumbo'. I discovered that the last-named had been so called ever since he was a baby, for the reason that when he was born he weighed 14-lb.

I was ordered to fall in with the rest of the gang, at the cabin, at 7 o'clock on Monday morning. There would be half-an-hour (8.30 to 9.00am) for breakfast, and three-quarters of an hour (1.00 to 1.45pm) for dinner, and 'knocking-off' time would be 5 o'clock. 'Jumbo' would make any tea and do any frying or heating up of our food. I was to bring ¼-lb tea, 1-lb sugar, a tin of condensed milk, and a knife and fork.

'Shall I bring a cup and saucer?' I asked.

'Not if you're *really* going to be one of us,' said Jim, the younger, 'We drink out of our tea cans, and there's a spare you can have. We also have an enamelled mug – a bit old and knocked about, perhaps, but it's clean.'

On Monday morning all hands were in the cabin a few minutes before seven. We opened our bags and red handkerchiefs and gave 'Jumbo' the victuals to be prepared for breakfast. Most consisted, as mine did, of a couple of rashers of bacon and an egg. On the stroke of seven, 'Ted', the ganger, said, 'Come on,' and we followed him out of the cabin – I to begin the hardest week's work of my life.

Sam's regular work is to sweep up the mileage yard, so he left us. 'Young Jim' went away to oil points. Ted gave us orders form our first job, and then went to examine his 'length'.

Under the protection of 'Joe', as look-out man, we started work on the 'down carriage road', taking off and oiling fish-plates. The 'oil' is a special mixture as black as tar and about as thick as treacle. In handling the oil fish-plates we got the stuff all over our hands and wrists, and in wiping the perspiration from our foreheads, it got onto our faces as well. We were like sweeps.

'Jumbo' left 'the job' a little before 8 o'clock, to go to the cabin to do the 'cooking'. Before partaking of our food we wiped our hands with some oily waste, to get the 'worst of it' off, and all washed them together in a bucket of water, drying them in a piece of old sacking which did duty as a towel.

I was glad of the enamelled mug, because the tea was too hot to drink out of the tea-can itself. We sat on a long wooden locker, on which too, we set our food, and during the meal we talked generally on any subject that happened to crop up.

The thing that struck me at once was the high level of the men's conversation. Their interest in the topics of the day, their intelligent views, and the extent of their general knowledge, were a revelation to me.

Only the brief mealtimes gave opportunities for learning something of the men themselves, as very little conversation took place 'on the job'. All that I discovered, however, was to the credit of the men. For example, I found that Ted, the ganger, is something of a scholar. He has no interests that take him out after his day's work, and he spends his evenings in study. Engineering subjects are his preference.

The elder Jim is a quiet little man. He contributes but little to the conversations, but when he speaks he says something that shows a ripe experience and a practical mind. He knows what's what. From the first, Jim made me feel sad. Afterwards I found that he was patiently carrying a heavy load of domestic trouble. For some years past his wife and family have had much more than their share of illness, and at the moment his wife was laid up and two of his children were in hospital.

'Jumbo', full of good humour, was three times wounded in the war. The one thing on his mind during my week with him was an effort with which he was cooperating, to raise money to give a seaside holiday to two hundred orphans and about as many widows. He breathes the spirit of human kindness.

Sam, too, works for others. Hospitals are his objective. He is a South Wales man and his wife and family are still in the Principality. He is every inch a philosopher. He thinks well before speaking, and then lets it bout in emphatic jerks. Now and then some of his longer words run away with him, but when they go too far he re-assembles the sentence, and has another shot at what he wants to say.

The younger Jim has a merry face and laughing eyes. He is all sunshine. He was 'look-out' man for the week, and my presence in the gang under his protection made him unusually serious. He felt the added responsibility. It was not that he thought my life was more precious than the lives of his other mates, but that if he managed to let me get run over, 'there'd sure be an awful row about it.'

Joe – the man of colour – is a real good sort.

'Jumbo' described him as having a black skin but a white heart. To me, Joe was all kindness. 'I'll look after you, Dick,' he said on my first day with the gang, and he was as good as his word.

The younger Jim's outside interests lie chiefly in his garden and allotment. He grows turnips that can beat all comers. Here and there on the sleepers and in the six-foot along our 'length', you might see the rings of various dimensions that have been scratched with pieces of ballast. These were drawn by Jim to show me the sizes of some of the turnips, onions and cabbages he had put into different shows.

A tall, slim, well-spoken and good-looking fellow is George. Culture is stamped upon him. He used to be in the Metropolitan Police, and I couldn't help feeling that he was far more suited to a position of that kind than to the work he is doing.

About the work itself I could write several pages. Suffice to say, at the moment, that from the point of view of the purpose I had in undertaking it, it was more successful than I had hoped. My 'boss' (the ganger) and all my mates were extremely helpful in every way.

After we had attended to the fishplates, we tightened fang bolts, replaced some broken ones, did some opening out, lifting of the lines, packing, slueing [More usually spelt as 'slewing', while to the workers it was known as 'pencil drill'], and filling in. We used jacks, rod-sets, an adze, a cross-cut saw, and other implements, handled sleepers and rail, replaced broken chairs, and did a number of other jobs. We were kept hard at work, except during intervals when – on the very welcome sound of Jim's whistle – we had 'to stand clear' for a train to pass over the line on which we were working. The Rule Book says that platelayers must stand clear immediately the look-out man blows his whistle. I obeyed the 'immediately' of that rule!

Never before had days seemed so long to me. The afternoons were simply endless. When walking from the job after finishing work the first evening, Jim told me that between 4.30 and 5 o'clock I had, by his counting, looked at my watch eighteen times, and twice had held it to my ear to hear if it was going! The heavy spanners and shovels of ballast were very different from the pen to which my hands had been accustomed, but I managed to avoid blisters by making a practice of holding a piece of waste in my hands when using the implements.

Towards the end of the week I felt used to the job, and found myself keenly interested in making the appropriately small pieces of ballast go tightly under the sleepers when we were 'taking out a slack'. I think that if I were a permanent way man for always, I should have real pride in making and keeping my lines in perfect condition. Indeed, this kind of pride seems to be a natural outcome of the work, for nothing struck me more forcibly than the painstaking and conscientious attitude of every man in the gang, towards every job that came his way.

There was one thing that pained me. It was that the platelayer is conscious of his grade being generally looked down upon and his work being held in small esteem. There was no grumbling, but plainly a feeling that, perhaps because of his hob-nailed boots, and dust-laden and oil-soaked clothes, he receives sparse consideration and scant respect. Speaking as I found him, the platelayer is a good sort, an excellent worker, and a splendid mate. And there is certainly a great deal more in his work than is commonly imagined.

It remains only to be said that within the big 'family' of Great Western workers, there is now a little circle of special friends, united by ties that will not easily be broken, and consisting of a Ted, two Jims, two Joes, a Sam, a George, a 'Jumbo', and a 'Dick'.

Clearly, there is a touch of condescension in this piece, even though the writer has high praise for those with whom he worked. It is also interesting in the amount of family detail involved, and the lack of any political correctness in dealing with Joe.

Checking the Tunnels

This is another piece that is written about a job, and a filthy and unpleasant one at that, by an 'outsider', one A.W. Marshall, writing in the *London & North Eastern Railway Magazine* about the important task of inspecting railway tunnels. The piece shows just how much attitudes to occupational health have changed, for the better, over the years, as one suspects that the chances of having a serious chest ailment amongst those handling this work in the steam age were very high. Notice again the lack of political correctness in the penultimate paragraph.

> In the majority of cases in this country, railway tunnels consist of an elliptical tube of brickwork, with small chambers (manholes) built into the sides at regular intervals, and, where possible, ventilating shafts from the roof to the outer air.
>
> At frequent intervals, almost invariably on Sundays, these tunnels are inspected … The inspection train consists of an engine, two low-sided goods wagons which carry a large number of oil flares, and the tunnel van. This latter rather resembles an ordinary goods brake, but has a flat roof, and iron ladder to gain access thereto, and a hinged platform at each side, which is drawn up when travelling from tunnel to tunnel.
>
> About Saturday midnight, dressed in their oldest clothes, the inspector and five or six men board the train. The guard gives 'right away', and off they go into the first tunnel.
>
> Just outside, the train halts, whilst the man responsible climbs into the wagon and lights up the flares: vile smelling things, these, but giving an abundance of light. The platform nearest the tunnel wall is lowered, and two men, armed with 6-foot poles

terminating in a steel prong, sit themselves on it. The remainder of the men go on the roof, some with long-handled hammers and some with the steel shod poles. All being ready, the train again moves forward; very slowly this time: not more than 2 or 3 miles per hour ... Tap! The leading man strikes the roof a sharp blow with his hammer, and then follows a succession of taps and thuds as the other hammers and prongs get to work, probing and sounding for any weak places. This continues all the way through the tunnel.

Soot falls in showers, and as the little train crawls further into the tunnel, the temperature rises, causing the perspiration to start and the soot to stick!

The inspector stands on the roof, with ears and eyes alert for the hollow ring that denotes a sinking of the brickwork, and for spaces between the bricks, which means that pointing is necessary.

Duck! Comes the warning shout from the leading man, and those on the van roof crouch low, as the tunnel roof, for the next 50 yards, is some 2 feet lower, and the man who forgets to 'duck' will find himself on the permanent way, some 14 feet below.

The inspector blows three short blasts on his whistle and the train stops. He has located a fault. The brickwork all round the suspected spot is scraped clear of soot, and a note made of the exact position and area, so that the necessary repairs can be effected in the near future. Suddenly there comes a continuous dripping sound, like rain, and in a few moments it is raining hard. This is only a wet portion of the tunnel where, owing to a spring or other underground water supply being tapped during construction, water is continually dripping through the brickwork.

Out in to the clean, fresh air at last, black as niggers, and with throats parched from the sulphur fumes which are always present in tunnels. But only one side of one tunnel has yet been examined. The train crosses over on to the other line and goes back again, the same procedures being adopted.

Then on to the next tunnel and the next, and the men will not return home until 5 o'clock or even later on Sunday afternoon, tired, dirty and thirsty, and if their first call is at the nearest 'pub' who can really blame them?

Definitely not one of the best jobs on the steam railway, and not at all glamorous, but nonetheless vital for not just the efficient working of the railway but for safety as well. Many tunnels encountered streams when they were built, leaving a permanent destructive presence behind their walls for the rest of their lives.

Life on the Line

Most of those who worked on the line lived at their homes, even if sometimes these were some distance away, but the LMS had an extensive network of lines in the sparsely-populated Scottish Highlands, and here the gangs of workmen had to live away from home in what were termed 'travelling dormitories'. These were no luxury sleeping cars, but an improvement on the tents first used. Old carriages that might have gone to scrap, or been converted into buildings in sidings and locomotive yards, used as holiday accommodation as 'camp coaches', or sold off to the public for various uses (sea front cottages, garden sheds and shelter and stores for shepherds, being but three), were converted as accommodation for workers.

The concept of the travelling dormitory was first used by the Highland Railway, one of the constituent companies of the LMS, and in its magazine, the LMS made the point that the Highland main line from Stanley Junction near Perth to Wick was 272 miles, almost the same as Euston to Carlisle. This is the *LMS Magazine* on the subject.

A good many years ago tents were used, but these were not altogether successful, and travelling dormitories made out of old carriages were tried and proved extremely satisfactory. These dormitories are fitted up with sleeping bunks complete with mattresses, pillows and blankets. A cooking stove is also provided together with such utensils as pots and pans, but the men of course provide their own food and arrange for the cooking of it amongst themselves. The external appearance of the dormitories may not be attractive, but it is extraordinary how comfortable living can be within. The usual duration of work in one place is not long and the men, therefore, seldom have to live in dormitories for an extended period. When there is a regular squad using the same van, such as the signal squad, the men take great pride in it, each man being responsible for his own kit. It may be said that during the winter there is as little work as possible done which necessitates the use of these travelling dormitories, the tradesmen at that time usually being engaged on work at or near towns.

Travelling dormitories, or 'vans' as the men call them, are also used in connection with bridge repairs on Sundays.

Men are sometimes taken long distances from Inverness and they travel, sleep and feed without leaving the 'van'. The 'van' in this case consists of a bogie carriage converted for that purpose. It contains sleeping accommodation for twelve men at one end, kitchen facilities in the centre and sleeping and living accommodation at the other end for the foreman and the inspectors. There is internal communication throughout and provision is made for the men getting their clothes dried in the event of bad weather.

During relaying or resleepering operations, dormitories are placed as near the work as possible. This method saves a great deal of time on the long single line sections as it is difficult to sandwich permanent way trains between the regular trains, particularly in the summer time. Altogether there are seventeen travelling dormitories on the Highland Section belonging to the engineering department.

Platelayers *versus* Drivers

This account from the *London & North Eastern Railway Magazine* came from one J.E. Rowett, writing when he was a stationmaster at Ryhall in Rutland. He was describing his early days on the railways, which seem to have been in the mid 1870s, when he started at the age of thirteen years as a lamp lad and junior platelayer working under his father, a foreman platelayer, on the line between Boston and Spalding. It seems clear that relationships between different categories of railwaymen were not all they should have been.

In those days candles were used in signal and gate lamps. The candles were supplied in packets which contained just the required number for one lamp for one month. The candles varied in length according to the season of the year, the candles for use in June being much shorter than those supplied for use in December, the explanation, of course, being that they would not be required to burn so long in the midsummer as in the shorter days of winter.

Train signalling by block telegraph had just been introduced, and it was my duty to attend to the distant signal lamps of a signal box that had been erected in a very lonely spot. My duties entailed a walk of three miles in either direction, and after I had walked six miles with the signal lamps I joined the plate-laying gang with whom I finished out the day. The signal box was closed weekends, and consequently I had to put out the distant signal lamps early Monday morning in readiness for the opening of the line at 6 o'clock. It was a lonely job, and in winter time not at all a joy ride. There were four levers in this box, and about twenty trains to deal with in twelve hours. The signalman, however, apparently thought that he was rather hard worked as he afterwards applied for an easier box. In after years, when working in a very busy main line signal box I often thought of that signalman in the lonely box in the heart of the countryside complaining of being over-worked.

The permanent way consisted of iron rails in sections 15-feet to 18-feet long. There were no fish plates, the two ends of adjoining rails being fastened in a 'joint chair' much larger than the standard chairs. Slag foundations [what we now know as ballast] were unknown in those days, and it was only to be expected that the line required considerable attention.

Everyone is aware of the great improvements effected in engines and rolling stock in recent years, but even then it is difficult to realise what travelling meant when carriages were roofless, and the seats quite innocent of any form of upholstery, whilst carriage springs had not by any means reached perfection. Needless to say, oscillation was not unknown, and consequently it had not become the custom to read the daily paper whilst travelling by train.

Engine drivers, although excellent men in their way, were not all noted for their consideration towards other grades of railwaymen, and some of them were very fond of playing practical jokes on the permanent way staff. It was customary for platelayers to carry with them a supply of keys and trenails usually in a large open basket, and a favourite prank of one particular driver, a gentleman from Doncaster, was to drop a lump of coal into the basket whilst passing by on his engine. He became so adept that he could score a 'bull's eye' every time, resulting in the keys and trenails flying in all directions, much to the dismay of the plate-layer. I remember one day my father and I were proceeding along the line, he with a bundle of straw on his back, when the same driver passed by on his engine. There was no basket for him to upset but he rose to the occasion by dropping a lump of blazing oily waste onto the straw. Fortunately, I was close behind and pulled the straw of my father's back. Another instance of the jocular mood of engine drivers in those days comes to mind. A gang of platelayers were about to proceed with their trolley to their home station about five miles away. A light engine was also going in the same direction and the driver offered to tow them home. The men gladly accepted his offer and the driver thereupon fastened their trolley to the engine tender by means of a cord, assuring them that he would not go too fast, and would put them down at their station. Off they went in fine style, but when they reached the station the driver showed no signs of pulling up, and appeared oblivious of his load. The foreman platelayer thereupon gave orders to cut the cord and so release the trolley, but after considerable effort the men found they could not do so as it was composed of wire. The driver had pity on them when they were five miles past their home station, and I do not think their thanks to him for his assistance were very cordial.

Chapter 11

Driving and Firing

Clearly, the glamour of engine driving was with those on the great expresses, and these men would be in what was known as the 'top link' of the engine shed or, in later years, motive power depot to which they were assigned. The link system provided a means of progression from driving a shunting locomotive through goods and stopping trains to semi-fast trains and then on to the expresses. A driver on the top link would be at the height of his profession, although he could be promoted to footplate inspector, the lower rung of operational management. Firemen also progressed through the same system, and then down again once promoted to driver.

The fireman had a harder and longer day than the driver if their first rostered locomotive of the day was starting from its shed. A few hours before the locomotive was needed, a firelighter would start a fire in order to raise steam, having first ensured that there was sufficient water in the tender or, if it was a tank engine, the tanks that could be either on either side of the boiler or on top of it, while some smaller locomotives would have the coal bunker on one side of the boiler and the water tank on the other. An hour before the locomotive was needed, the fireman would turn up and see that the fire was sufficient and that steam was raised, ready for the driver.

Of course, it was much easier to take over a locomotive en route, say at Carlisle for an Anglo-Scottish express, which thanks to larger tenders and water troughs could see the same locomotive running all the way from London to Edinburgh or Glasgow. The work involved was considerable. An express tender could have between 4,000 and 5,000 gallons of water, but more significant for the fireman was that running nonstop from King's Cross to Edinburgh Waverley would need up to 7½ tons of coal to be moved from the tender to the firebox manually by the fireman. Not surprisingly, the London & North Eastern Railway introduced corridor tenders on these services so that the footplatemen could be changed during the long and arduous journey.

Not all steam locomotives had the luxury of a driver and fireman. The Romney Hythe & Dymchurch Railway had locomotives handled by one man, as we will see. The LNER experimented with a tank engine with mechanical coaling using two helical devices to move the coal from the bunker to the firebox, and although technically successful, this project was not taken further due to objections from the trades unions. It has to be remembered, however, that while the union attitude might have appeared Luddite, at the time there were no failsafe devices on steam locomotives to compare with the so-called 'dead man's handle' on electric rolling stock. On the other hand, on some railways, including the Romney, Hythe & Dymchurch, locomotives were of necessity handled by a driver on his own combing the duties of driver and fireman.

While the glamour of engine driving belongs to the prestigious expresses manned by the 'top link' of drivers and firemen at a major depot, much of the hardest and most demanding work was done by those on suburban duties, especially on short distance stopping trains with no chance to recover time lost and with short, but demanding, turnrounds at stations. These services were usually worked by powerful tank engines, which could run equally well forwards and backwards, whereas tender locomotives would usually back out of the station to a turntable before returning to take a later train.

A First Turn at Firing

G.C. Potts, who had started earlier with the Great Central Railway in Yorkshire, had spent two years as a cleaner and then a further three years on duties such as fire bar laying, before vacancies arose for firemen, provided that the applicants passed a test with the locomotive inspector. This was 1927, and after the General Strike of the previous year there was a short-lived improvement in trade; and all of his peers passed as firemen with him. The newly-qualified were not put on the road immediately, but had to wait their turn, initially as a relief, and the length of time they spent before this happened depended on their seniority. Meanwhile, they were kept at their existing duties, although restless and waiting to move on, prompting one of the cleaners' foremen to say: 'Another dozen bloody good cleaners spoilt now they are passed out!'

As it happened, Potts recalled that he didn't have to wait too long before his first shift as a fireman.

I had booked on at 2.00pm and happened to be the senior cleaner; fortunately for me a fireman had gone sick and I was told by the foreman cleaner to go to the enginemen's room and report. There I was given instructions by the Running Foreman to go to engine 5386 ... working the Moorhouse-Herculanean Docks. Hell, I thought to myself, this sounds important! So I asked rather diffiently who my driver was and he said with a slight smile, 'Bill Hooper – and he eats three passed cleaners for his breakfast, so hurry up and get out of the shed!'

I hurried to the mess room for my snap tin and coat, then to the lamp stores for headlamps and a firing shovel. I saw on the engine board that the engine I wanted was outside the shed on No. 6 road, so off I went to find it. This didn't take a moment and I put my headlamps in the position for light engine, put my coat and tin in the cupboard and then introduced myself to the driver, who was oiling the eccentrics in the motion. When he came out from between the frames ... he looked at me and said, 'What do they call thee? Has tha been out afore?' I told him who I was and added that this was going to be my first firing shift. 'Bloody hell, I do gerram! Anyhow, has tha fetched tools?' I shook my head, somewhat dumstruck. 'Tha better fetch 'em then.' Having hurried back from this little errand, I started to sweep the footplate up, clean the gauge glasses and check that we had a full complement of fire irons ... [These included long and short shovels, straight and bent darts or pokers, brushes.]

I was fortunate that the steam gauge showed 100-lbs as I was late ... The allowance time for preparing ... was one hour from signing on to being booked out at the Top Pit cabin ...

We left the depot and trundled through Mexborough station toward Denaby Crossing but we came to a stand at the home signal ... after waiting the prescribed time I proceeded to the signal box to carry out Rule 55, which meant protection by the signalman ... I informed the bobby ['Bobby', an old term for signalmen dating from the early days when trains were controlled by railway company police.] where we stood, where we were going and asked if he had protected us.

This account gives a good idea of how much work was needed before a steam locomotive could move, and Potts was amazed to learn from his driver that they might not be going very far in their shift, largely because it would be a coal train and everything else took precedence over it, so they had to wait their turn to join the main line and could expect to be diverted into sidings to allow passenger trains and express freights to pass.

A Day on the Suburban Footplate

One of the busiest suburban networks was that from Liverpool Street on the LNER, and the *London & North Eastern Railway Magazine* carried a lengthy piece by Driver J.W. Barnes who drove a Stratford-based 0-6-2T locomotive. While some railways or depots tried to give a driver the same locomotive all of the time, perhaps with a relief driver for the other half of the day's diagram, this was rare. Barnes was allocated a locomotive on starting in the morning, but on a later shift he would take over a locomotive already 'in steam' or in service from another driver. He soon makes it clear that the job has lost its glamour as far as he is concerned. As it took time to raise steam, firelighters would have started the job some time before the driver and fireman reported for duty, leaving the fireman to complete the job.

> The work of a driver on the suburban passenger services on our railway may not be so spectacular as that of a driver of an express train travelling, say, from King's Cross to York, and onwards, but it is just as exacting and, shall I say, at time a little more monotonous. He signs on duty at any time during the twenty-four hours as required and prepares the engine (if he is on the morning turn) before commencing the day's work.
>
> After signing on duty I have to consult the duty list to find out my diagram working and the number of the engines booked to me. The various notices and instructions posted in the Notice Lobby have to be examined and any alterations or additions noted, after which I proceed to the engine.
>
> In the meantime, the fireman has proceeded to the stores for the engine tools and the supply of oil for the day.
>
> On joining the engine I look at the water gauge glass to satisfy myself that the water level in the boiler is correct, and I then proceed to examine fusible plugs and tubes. My next job is to

oil-up the big ends, and straps, slide blocks, small ends, side rods and axle boxes are all carefully examined and oiled. The lubricators are filled and the Westinghouse [the name of an equipment manufacturer, in this case of air brakes, but his locomotive also uses the vacuum brake] pump (if the engine is Westinghouse fitted) examined and oiled. I then proceed to examine the fittings in the smokebox.

While I am doing this, the fireman is busy performing his side of the work of preparation. He first of all prepares the fire so as to ensure a full head of steam, and afterwards fills the tanks with water. He then examines and cleans the destination and disc boards and satisfies himself that he has the correct boards for the day's work. He examines and cleans the head lamps, at the same time seeing that they are well supplied with oil and wick. The sand boxes are then fitted up and the gear tested; the smokebox door is tried to ensure that it is securely fastened. The coal in the bunker has to be broken up and safely stacked so that no coal is likely to fall from the bunker. The fire-irons are then safely stacked and the engine tools stowed away, and having tested the Westinghouse and vacuum brakes, we are ready to leave the shed.

Our destination is governed by the diagram working; sometimes we proceed to one of the numerous carriage sidings and work an empty carriage train to the appropriate station for passenger train working, and at other times we may proceed light to, say, Liverpool Street, to take up passenger train working.

The working of suburban passenger train service in the Stratford District is arranged by headquarters by means of engine rosters or diagrams, and below is an example of one of these diagrams.

On duty 4.10am
  5.05am, light engine to Loughton
  6.23am, Loughton to Liverpool Street
  7.39am, Liverpool Street to Ilford
  8.24am, Ilford to Liverpool Street
  9.17am, Liverpool Street to Ilford
10.23am, Ilford to Fenchurch Street
11.54am, Fenchurch Street to Woodford via Fairlop
  1.50pm, Woodford to Ilford

3.31pm, Ilford to Woodford

4.22pm, Woodford to Snaresbrook

5.10pm, Snaresbrook to Ilford

5.53pm, Ilford to Fenchurch Street

6.46pm, Fenchurch Street to Chadwell Heath

7.48pm, Chadwell Heath to Ilford

8.30pm, Ilford to Woodford

9.50pm, Woodford to Ilford

11.23pm, Ilford to Woodford

12.00, light engine to Stratford Shed

Seventy-seven of these diagrams are necessary to cover the engines working the suburban trains on any one day at Stratford. The working at the Stratford depot is divided into what are called 'links' and the diagrams vary according to the link we may be working in. I have been through all these links and have worked at some time or other on all the various suburban services of the Stratford depot – including the intensive service on the Enfield and Walthamstow lines – incidentally this service is known to the enginemen as the 'Jazz' service [The pre-grouping Great Eastern was amongst the first to use distinctive stripes to identify classes, with first having yellow lines and second blue, which earned them the title of the 'Jazz Trains'. It was rare for services to have three classes at this time, but this continued under the LNER.], but how it got its nickname is another story.

Our suburban trains are booked to the half-minute, and it is essential to watch carefully these half-minutes as any overlooking may result in delays not only to our train but to the trains following us, and as the working at Liverpool Street is so intensive in the peak period, we might, by being even a minute late, delay the outgoing train and thus tend to disorganise the traffic at a critical time of day.

It is very important when bringing the engine to rest at Liverpool Street, that we stop directly opposite the water column so as to enable us to take water whilst the passengers are joining the outwards train. As the train goes out of the platform, we have to be ready to follow it down the platform and proceed at once into the engine dock so as to clear the platform road for the passage of the next inwards train.

In addition to noting which trains we should work, it is also necessary for us to look up the trains in the Working Time Table and make note of the stations at which the train is booked to call, and should we run past a station instead of stopping, or stop at a station at which we are not booked, we have to answer for it by going 'on the carpet'. It is interesting to note here that in the diagram quoted above that are 134 'stops', of course the more serious of these errors is the former, as naturally there are passengers waiting to join the train, and by our omission it may mean that some business man may lose an appointment which might result in serious financial loss to him. The Rule Book, Appendix to the Working Time Tables, and Green Relaying Notices, must also be studied, and all applicable instructions have to be carried out.

The varying gradients of the road have to be memorised, and the working of the engine adapted to the variations. Signals also have to be kept in mind and their positions and names remembered.

If there are no untoward happenings, we pursue the even tenor of our way through the diagram working and finish our day's work at the appointed time. If, however, the weather becomes foggy, or anything happens to put the engines out of their rostered working, a very different tale has to be told. It is then that we have to 'look to our laurels' and be prepared for any emergency, often having to work trains to destinations much different to that to which we should work in our diagrams.

It is also most essential that we watch the work of our fireman when he is firing the engine, to see that no excessive emission of smoke occurs and there is no waste by the engine 'blowing off'. At the same time it is most important to maintain full steam pressure and to use an engineman's phrase, 'keep the old engine on the red line.'

At the end of the day's work the engine returns to the locomotive depot, and even then the driver's work is not finished. He has to 'dispose' of his engine. The work of disposal is just as important as the task of preparation. After arrival on the disposal pit the driver leaves the engine to consult the duty list, and instructs the fireman not to move the engine until he returns.

The driver reports to the running foreman for instructions as to the disposal; he then consults the duty list to see if the engine is required for further service that date or if it is booked for boiler-washing or repairs; if the engine is required for further service, the driver looks at the diagram working so as to know how much coal he should have placed in the bunker when he arrives as the mechanical coaling plant. On his return to the engine at the disposal pit, he goes under the leading end of the engine, examines the steam chest and cylinder cover studs and nuts, the piston and spindle, gland nuts and studs, the small end pins and cross-head cotters and split pins; he examines the link motion, taper pins, etc., all fore and back gear straps, fork and butt end nuts and pins, sheaves and big ends. After satisfying himself that they are in good order and cotters tight and split cotters properly split and in position, he will feel the axle boxes and big end brasses for any signs of possible heating, and examines all springs, etc. He examines the brake gear and connections and afterwards proceeds around the outside of the engine examining the wheels, brake block and hangers and side rods. He then mounts the footplate and examines the fittings on the 'front' including the lubricators, and connections, etc. The Westinghouse and vacuum and steam heating fittings, the smokebox for leaky joints, the firebox, brick arch and tubes are also examined, and any necessary repairs noted, to be entered afterwards on the repairs sheet.

After the fireman has completed his work of drawing the fire, cleaning the ashpan and smokebox from ashes, the engine is taken to the coaling plant, stopping on the way to allow the fireman to take the bucket containing the engine tools into the stores.

After the engine has been coaled, it proceeds to the shed, where all lamps and disc boards are removed and placed on the irons inside the cab.

Should the driver receive instructions from the running foreman that the fire is to be left in, he should, before leaving the engine in the shed, see that the boiler is filled, the fire is under the brick arch and that the dampers are closed. He is then free to go home, provided that he has completed his rostered turn of duty and that the foreman has no further duties for him.

Romney, Hythe & Dymchurch

P. Ransome-Wallis was not a railwayman, although he had wanted to become one but instead family pressures led to him studying medicine. He nevertheless indulged his ambition vicariously by becoming a noted railway photographer and writer, but he was especially famed for his photography. In early summer 1946, he volunteered to drive locomotives on the 15-inch gauge Romney, Hythe & Dymchurch Railway, desperately short of drivers after the end of the Second World War. The line was also in a shocking state, having been used, or misused, by the British Army during the war years when it was used to supply coastal artillery units, and even had its own armoured and armed train.

Typical of the damage done during the war years was that the interlocking frame at New Romney had been smashed by a sledge hammer as the soldier in the signalbox had not been given training on how to clear signals. The line beyond New Romney to Dungeness was still waiting to be repaired after its wartime neglect, so services could only be operated between New Romney and Hythe.

Ransome-Wallis was trained on one of the RH&D' nine locomotives operational at the time, two of which were based on Canadian examples, albeit with Canadian Pacific locomotives allied to Canadian National tenders. Confusingly, the Canadian Pacific locomotives were indeed Pacifics, that is with a 4-6-2 wheel configuration. Ransome-Wallis was taught on one of these, No. 10, named *Dr Syn*. Both men fitted comfortably in the cab for training, despite the narrow gauge.

If anyone thinks that to drive one of these little engines is all fun ... he is very much mistaken ... it is one of the hardest day's work I can ever remember. You start early, preparing your engine – get the fire going, fill up lubricators, oil all round, and clean off the paintwork and side rods, to name but a few items. Off the shed at New Romney, on to your first train, and away you go to Hythe. Arrived there – off the train, back on the turntable, get water and coal as needed, fill up the lubricators, set-back onto the train and soon you are away again to New Romney ... If you are lucky you will get about forty minutes on the shed at lunchtime to consume some much-needed food! After twelve hours of it you are glad to call it a day!

His usual load was eight carriages, and he soon became used to sightseers pointing at the 'toy engine' and asking: 'Has it really got a fire in it?' or 'Does the whistle blow?' and, perhaps worst of all: 'Isn't it sweet?' R.-W. found some of these remarks nauseating. Fortunately, whistles were being blown on the platform and it was time to go.

I open the regulator gently without a trace of slip I ease the train out of the station ... Look around the cab – steam pressure, vacuum, water level in the gauge glass – all in order and the engine picking up nicely. Soon I bring back the reverser, notching up 30 per cent, and then giving her a little more steam, the regulator more than half open. She responds beautifully ... I open the firedoor; there are two or three blow-holes developing and I cover them up with a few well-placed shovels of coal, making sure before I do that there are no overbridges in sight. Some of these are very low and if, while firing. I raise my head above the level of the cab when we pass under one I am liable to be knocked out for a very long time! Level crossing ahead – shut off steam, reverser to drifting position and a long loud blast on the chime whistle [A North American feature fitted for authenticity, serving the same function as a whistle.], while I bring down the vacuum and brake gently to a walking pace, keeping a good look-out all the while. All clear and I open up again. I make the stop at Dymchurch ... and ... *Dr Syn* starts blowing off gently, impatient to be away. Off we go, steaming over the marshes at 30 mph, the engine riding well, steaming well, and I soon find myself confidently a part of the whole set-up. Firing, injectors, level-crossings, whistle – I begin to take them all in my stride, all the time keeping a keen look-out on the road ahead and remembering those places where special caution is needed ... down the gentle gradient towards the terminus at Hythe. I shut off, and make a gentle brake application to 'get hold' of the train. For too great a brake application may cause the wheels to 'pick up' and I could find *myself* with the train sliding down the gradient with wheels locked out of control.

Driving the Pumping Engine

The infrastructure of the railways required much support, including pumping engines to keep some of the tunnels free of water, while others pumped water for use by the railway's locomotives. It is not clear whether this pumping engine article in the *LMS Magazine*, written by 'S.B.' refers to such an engine, probably the latter, but it does show another side to working with the steam engine. He seems to work single-handed.

The pumping engine is older than the locomotive itself. It was early pressed into the service of the railway and pumping plants still function on railways all over the country doing their part towards the successful conduct of the great transport under-takings which mean so much to us all. Most likely their existence is unknown to the thousands who daily use the iron road for transport of themselves or their freight. Very probably many railwaymen, too, have never given them a thought, but there they are, quite as important in their way as other units of the railway system more prominently in the public eye.

The plant of which I am in charge is operated by steam gener-ated in a Cornish type boiler at a working pressure of 80-lb, which sounds little enough, I know, when compared with a 'Royal Scot', but is nevertheless sufficient for its purpose. When I take over duty, my first care is to see that all is in perfect working order, just as my colleague the engine driver does, and with critical eye I carefully examine every part of my charge, doing whatever oiling, etc., is necessary. We have continually to watch that steam pressure is kept up and that the level of water in the tank is maintained. In my case the tank is a mile away, and there is a wonderful electrical contrivance in the engine house which indi-cates the level of water in the tank, and rings a bell if it is full or empty. By means of this indicator we know how to regulate the steam in the boiler so as to have just what is required and not waste coal by keeping up a bigger fire than is really wanted.

As soon as my steam pressure gauge shows I have the neces-sary pressure, and the tank wants filling, I open the steam wheel, which is on the same principle exactly as the steam regulator of my colleague on the locomotive, and I let the engine run a short while with the taps open so as to clear the cylinders of water. Then I close the taps, give the steam wheel another turn, and listen for the sound of the pump which lifts the water from the river and drives it through the mile of pipe to the tank. An experienced man can tell in several ways whether the pump is acting properly. But the simplest is by the sound the engine makes. This is a very helpful guide, because your duties take you out of the engine house from time to time, but not beyond earshot of your engine, so you can always tell at once how things are going, even when the various gauges are temporarily out of sight.

Suppose, for instance, you hear the engine running fast. This means she has not got sufficient work to do, in other words that she is not pumping water, so off you go to find the reason and put the matter right. Knowing that there is nothing wrong with the pumps or packing, you at once conclude that something is happening to choke the water supply, which often occurs where I am if there has been a storm and the river is flooded. Because then all sorts of debris gets carried downstream, and probably the rose at the end of the intake valve has got blocked up with leaves and mud which form a barrier the water cannot penetrate. So then you put on the thigh-boots you are provided with and wade into the stream to clear the obstruction, and almost certainly you will hear your engine rapidly recover its normal stride, telling you in unmistakable language that the pumps have got their proper work to do once more.

At lot depends on the way you fire the boiler. It wants constant attention and intelligent handling to get the best results with the maximum economy. You have first of all to consider the quality of the coal; then there is the strength of the blast, and the quantity of fuel in the firebox. Generally speaking it is essential that the fire should be as thin as possible without being allowed to burn into holes; but it must be somewhat thicker at the sides than in the centre. This allows free access of air to all parts, and prevents any tendency of the gases to creep up the plates and pass out through the tubes before they have been properly consumed. I devote a great deal of time and care to getting the best possible results from my boiler.

Frosty weather ... brings special troubles for the pump engine-man. The cranes that supply water for the engines are liable to get frozen, and it is one of our duties to see this does not happen. In my case, as I have already said, the tank and crane are a full mile away, so I rely on the signalman, whose box is close at hand, to ring me up in case of emergency. But of course the right thing is to be prepared, so if there is any likelihood of severe frost I go without being called. In either case it means I shall be away from my engine for a considerable time, so first I see the boiler is quite full, draw my fire to the front, close down the dampers and shut off the steam. When this is done and I am satisfied that all is safe, I get away as quickly as I can, and light the crane fires with sticks that are provided. I examine it carefully to see there are no burst pipes, allowing a flush of water to run through to satisfy myself that all is well before I get back to the pumping station to carry on.

Usually, the economy of diesel or electric working is seen as having one less man on the locomotive footplate, but this clearly shows that there were other manpower costs as well to keep the steam railway working.

Chapter 12

Sticking Up for the Company

Strangely, twice the *London & North Eastern Railway Magazine* felt that it was important to let its readers know about the role of the billposter. These were, of course, the days before advertising on radio while television did not appear until the late 1930s, and then only in the London area and it was to be many years before what was at first known as commercial television was to appear. Newspaper advertising was used, but then, as now, local newspaper advertising is very expensive for the number of people reached and has the added costs of tailoring advertisements to the circulation area. It is not surprising that posters were important. The Southern Railway even held a competition for the best chalked blackboards announcing excursions or cheap day tickets. Even British Railways used blackboards, and these worked. Once getting off the ferry from Portsmouth at Ryde with two cousins, I was attracted by a blackboard notice offering cheap day returns to the main stations on the busy line to Ventnor, and immediately forgot my mother's insistence that we didn't go beyond Ryde as I have always liked Ventnor!

The first LNER piece was signed by a certain William Stead, the billposter at Glasgow's Queen Street Station, but the second was unsigned, and all the reader was told was that the individual concerned was a 'Company's Billposter in the N.E. Area', which meant somewhere between York and the Scottish Border.

The 'Art of Sticking Up'

Accompanied by a number of small cartoons showing the tribulations of a billposter's life, the earlier piece attempted to make the most of the role and even to glamorise it to some extent.

> The billposter nowadays is a very important unit in the working of a railway. He has to be much more than a mere hanger of paper on a billboard. For instance, he must have an eye for a straight

line, which sometimes takes a great deal of practice to acquire, and he must be able to recognise the difference in the quality of paper as the stretching of one quality is entirely different from another. On working pictorial posters on a board that handles more than one he must endeavour to work out a colour scheme, for unless the colours harmonise then the best effect is lost, and this reduces the value of the poster as an effective advertisement.

The billposter has quite a lot to contend with in the course of an ordinary day's work, as weather conditions, wind, rain and frost all go to make it more difficult for him to carry out his duties, and each change in the weather must be met by a different method of working. When posting a bill on a windy day the billposter must be able to use both hands efficiently so that he can get the bill pasted down on the windward side first, and it very often happens that before it has been properly fixed an old lady will stop and ask particulars of some excursions, and while trying to gratify a prospective customer's thirst for information, a very playful wind has carried the bill about half a mile up the street, and the job has to be started all over again. The second attempt is usually more successful; possibly because of what the billposter has been thinking about the interruption (as there is a policeman at the corner, he can't afford to think loudly or the Company may be short of his services for a few days).

Frosty weather is a great setback unless salt has been added to the paste, for in a very hard frost the paste freezes on the board before the bill can be placed in position ... if the bill is allowed to freeze on the board, it will drop off when the temperature rises.

A Day in the Life ...

The second piece seems set to further enhance the reputation of the billposter, but one also suspects that it was someone trying to show how clever they had been in providing new and more legible summary bills, each announcing a number of excursions or special offers rather than leaving these to a succession of smaller bills. Of course, one advantage of this move was that the credibility of any bill or poster board is much reduced if out of date material is left on display. That seems so basic, but it also applies even to the Internet today, when details of last year's Christmas offers are still on display the following summer!

'Yours is a soft job, nothing to do but walk around in the sunshine and stick up a few bills.' So often have I been told this, though perhaps not in so many words, that I feel, in justice to myself and other members of the Company's staff doing similar work, some attempt should be made to set out what really has to be done before a full display of bills can be placed in front of the thousands of people who live in the North Eastern Area and have for so many years been taught to look for details of cheap rail travel on boards in the town.

Mine is not a soft job, nor is it always done in sunshine – more often rain these past few years. I start work at 8.00 in the morning and my first job until quite recently was to sort out up to fifteen or more different kinds of handbills to be posted on each board I go to, about forty-two, so I have forty-two sets of bills of fifteen or more, 630 bills in all. Next I have to mix some paste sticky enough to keep the bills on the boards in all weathers, and it varies very much in my district. This done, with my bills in my bag, my paste can, which is divided – one half to hold clean water and one half to hold paste; my brushes and my scraper, weighing all told about 2 stones, I set off.

Most of the town boards which come under my care were made for sixty small bills measuring 6¼ inches by 10 inches, but bills double this size have to be posted occasionally. I attend to the boards in rotation on a route which has been planned out. I carefully examine every bill on each board to see which has fallen out of date since my last visit, wash all such bills down by soaking them with water and then scraping them off – not an easy job when in winter the water freezes as you put it on – and great care must be taken not to damage the surface of the boards when using the scraper. Fifteen or more bills have often to be scraped off from different parts of the board, and if I do not wish to give myself extra work, I must remove them without damaging any of the other bills. Having got the bills off, I have to post the fresh ones, again using care so they do not show creases or be smeared or they will not be passed by the Inspector. Then, lastly, I must clear up all scraps of bills from the foot of the board, otherwise *I shall soon have the Police after me.* Not until I have done this at all the forty-two boards, which takes me two days from 8.00am to 5.00pm, can I say I have finished, and when you know the route round all the boards is about twenty miles I think you will have to admit I have not such a soft job after all.

Just recently a larger bill measuring 12 inches by 30 inches, and giving full particulars of excursions running during one week has been brought out in my district. This does away with a lot of sorting and some posting, as I have now to stick up only one bill for each week, although I have still to show bills advertising rail facilities other than excursions.

Billposting, although it is the way I earn my living, is not the most interesting part of my day's round. As a billposter, I ought to be best able to talk about the use made of the boards and from what I see each day, I know that they are most useful and save many people having to walk a long way to the station. Old ladies particularly being very thankful for this.

The new summary bills now in use are much better than so many small bills, and people have told me when at the boards that this idea should have been thought of long ago, because it is now so simple to find what you are looking for and the larger type makes them so much easier to read.

Interesting to note that there was mention of freezing weather, but not of mixing salt with the paste, or the water. Perhaps his colleague in Glasgow had kept this trade secret to himself. At the time, his round would have been made on foot, or just possibly by bicycle, but certainly he would not have had the benefit of a van, unlike today.

Chapter 13

In the Signal Box

One of the most demanding and responsible jobs on the railways was that of the signalman, although the responsibilities varied considerably with some working on quiet branch lines with only two or three trains a day, and others being part of a team in a busy box at a major junction. Between the world wars, shifts were reduced considerably with the widespread introduction of an eight hour day, which one railway general manager criticised, pointing out that the demands on a signalman on a quieter line were nothing compared with those at a busy junction. Before this, twelve hour days were not uncommon.

We start with a junior role, but one that was important and illustrated how the LMS adopted the Midland Railway's system of train control and extended it. This was a system that was over and above the signal boxes and enabled them to function efficiently.

The Telephone Attendant

This role was another component in the system of signalling and control of the railway, and comes from the *LMS Magazine*'s 'Juniors Page', although it extended over more than one page. It was signed by a young man, F.P. Saunders, who was based at Bletchley.

> To begin with, I work in the Telegraph Office. My job is practically the same as the signal-cabin lads, differing only in that we do telegram work and they don't. I have also told them that we do a lot more, but they won't have it! The idea of our work is that I receive reports of certain trains from different places, and telephone the information forward to the signal-boxes for regulating purposes. I wonder how many people realise that I, and my mates, know where practically every train is between Rugby on one side and Tring on the other! This comprises my telephone area. Of course, we actually have a much wider range; it really stretches from Willesden to Coventry and Nuneaton, but from

these kind of places we really only do a kind of skeleton booking, The idea is that the telephone attendant at Tring wires an express as passing him at, say, 1.20am, I in turn telephone it to Bletchley No. 2 cabin, Roade, and Northampton or Blisworth.

If you know anything about the main line, you know that it branches at Roade Junction. The left-hand fork, known as the 'old' line, goes north via Blisworth, and the right-hand one, or 'new' line, swings out north-eastward, passing through Northampton and linking up with the old line again at Rugby. It follows then that care has to be taken which way the trains are wired. For instance, suppose the lad at Tring wires me an express which is timed old line. What happens if I inadvertently wire it new line? Perhaps there is an empty wagon train waiting in the sidings at Roade to go old line, and the signalman at Roade, thinking the express just wired is for Northampton, turns the empty wagon train out to jog along to Blisworth. A minute or so afterwards he has the express offered by the next signal cabin, but for the old line instead of for Northampton, and the consequence is the express is continually delayed at signals by the empty wagon train in front.

The same might easily occur if the train lad forgot to report a train at all; but of course, in practice, such things hardly happen once in a lifetime, although I do remember one case where a certain lad stopped the 'Ulster Express' at Bletchley seven minutes!

When you realise that three of us boys do about 2,000 train reports in twenty-four hours you will see what we have to cope with. It isn't only passenger trains we deal with, but every train. Empty wagons, express freight, mineral – in fact, all the trains on the main line.

The control office is next door to us, and all the trains we receive we book on a sheet which the regulator can see through a window. From this sheet he can tell where all the trains are, and so regulate them. The regulator tells the signalmen what to do with the trains; whether to send one fast or slow line, whether to put one in the 'loop' to let another one by, and so on. Of course, that is but a particle of what all he does, but I think that he could explain it a lot better than I can. To get back to my own job, however. I receive a train report from Nuneaton or Coventry, and book it on the control sheet only. Then the same train from Rugby I send to No. 2 Box, Tring and Willesden. From Blisworth I report it to Tring, from Roade to Bletchley No. 2 and from No. 2 to Tring and Watford. Then the lad at Tring wires it forward when it passes him. In this way, you see, every train is continually under supervision by somebody.

The same process is carried out in the opposite direction, or 'downhill', as we know it.

We write all our own train sheets out, which number fifty-two on the night shift and not quite so many on the afternoon or morning shifts.

Our lads spend about five or six years as telephone attendants, and are moved out of the telegraph office when they are 20. During that time we learn telegraphy quite well, and can be of material assistance to the telegraph clerks when necessary. They in turn prove to be good pals by helping us all they can when we get out of our depth. I think a spirit of harmony means everything in a big office. Of course, telephone work is not all we do. We deliver telegrams on the station, clean the office regularly, get the coal in, and scrub the floor on Friday morning. And believe me, with the odour of soft soap continually in your nose and splinters in your fingers, it is none too pleasant a job!

Learning the Ropes

As mentioned later in Chapter 16, one of the greatest railwaymen was Sir Felix Pole of the Great Western Railway, who joined the company in 1891 and was appointed general manager in 1921, which meant that an important task was preparing the company for grouping in 1923. None of the 'Big Four' achieved grouping as well as the GWR, and while some of this is to Pole's credit, it is also true that the GWR dominated the other constituent companies in a way that no other company could at grouping and was, after all, the only one of what Parliament termed the 'Western group of companies' with a London terminus. Not the least of his achievements was ensuring that the Great Western name survived as the politicians would have preferred a new title.

Nevertheless, he too had to work his way up and this is his account of time spent in a signal box.

When I started at Swindon it was the custom there, and at some other large places, for the junior telegraph clerks to divide their time between the telegraph office and one or other of the signal boxes. I was allocated to 'D' box, and my working hours were from 8.30am until 9.00pm, with a couple of meal intervals. Each day the juniors worked for two brief periods in the main telegraph office, with the object of training them in telegraph office duties.

In the signal box the work consisted of sending and receiving code messages for shunting operations. There is no doubt that the direct association with the working of traffic was of great educational value. It was also instructive to be associated with the signalman in a large and busy box.

In 'D' box I came under the influence of a young, keen, energetic man named Cullen, who finished his career as an inspector at Cardiff. Cullen was a real sergeant-major and required a high standard of service. Years later – in 1924 – when making a presentation to Mr Cullen on his retirement, I said:

"I am going to tell a story about an event which happened over thirty years ago. On commencing service at Swindon, my work took me into a large signal box. This was worked by three men, each of whom did an eight hour turn of duty – all non-conformists who never indulged in bad language. In later years I realised that they represented three classes of employees.

"No. 1 was an excellent signalman, knew the rules thoroughly, but was not greatly interested in the working of the traffic other than in his own section.

"No. 2 was a lazy fellow, who lost many half-minutes because he was sitting down when a bell rang or was looking out of the window discussing some political or other subject. Later on, he had to leave the service.

"No. 3 was the embodiment of all one could expect from a keen signalman. He always arrived a little before his turn of duty was due to commence and quickly ascertained, by well directed questions, how the trains were working. All his efforts were directed to speeding trains by saving time wherever possible, thereby getting the business done in a first-class manner. Not only that, but he was ambitious, and properly so. He was out to progress in the Great Western service; he desired to become an inspector and to take an even more important part in the company's operations; he had a good influence on those around him.

"I might pursue this story further, but I think I have said enough to indicate who No. 3 was – our old friend William Cullen."

The Day's Work

The first piece is unsigned, other than by 'One of Them'. He is one of three signalmen sharing shifts at a box which covers a junction, which is busy, but not on a par with, say, Newcastle or York. This comes from the *London & North Eastern Railway Magazine*.

Once again I vaulted the fence and trod the familiar path leading to the signalbox. I reflected, with some satisfaction, that of the three who manned the box, I alone was able to vault that fence. Jack and Bill, now middle-aged, were content to negotiate the obstacle one leg at a time.

As I approached the box, Jack appeared at the window, exhibiting a green flag. 'Hello,' I cried, 'things going all right?' 'None too well, Tom,' was the reply. 'The fasts are running late, generally appearing on the scene on the timing of a branch passenger train. Have had to hold branch trains at the outer [outer signal, or distant, as opposed to the home signal]. Am fed up writing delay notes. Dash that driver! Why doesn't he answer my caution signal? Ah, at last, give him the starting [starter, or starting signal, indicating to the driver of a train that he may move], Tom, while I count his train for the control.' Jack, evidently, had been having a harassing time. Timing at this junction is so close that the late running of one train can affect adversely the running of three others. Such happenings bring anxious moments to the signalman on duty. Quick and accurate judgement is necessary if the best running is to be got out of the margins available. Having furnished me with all the particulars enabling me to take up the threads, Jack departed for home and a well-earned meal.

The block instruments are now clear, and this being a quiet period likely to remain so for the next ten minutes, I will take the opportunity of describing the duties that lie ahead of me until the clock strikes ten. The frame is comparatively small, there being thirty levers. There are three sets of block instruments and bells, three telephones (the buzzing of which provides a never-ending accompaniment to the clattering of levers and the ringing of bells), and a telegraph instrument that seems to choose the most awkward times for sounding my station call. There are points and one distant signal that require special attention as they are operated on the semi-automatic principle. Nine track indicators have to be kept under observation, and last, but by no means least, a train register in which an average of eleven trains an hour is entered. I need not dwell on the importance of this book. Suffice to say that, at junctions, particularly, it constitutes a very important log of the day's work. Our average of eleven trains per hour gives an assessment of 200 'marks' per hour. One could be busier, much busier. Many boxes have an assessment of 400 'marks' per hour, but are, as a rule, manned by additional signalmen.

I have already mentioned the persistency of the telegraph instrument, or to be more exact, the telegraph clerk at the other end of the line. Not a little of our trouble is caused by his reluctance to take seriously our 'MQ' or 'SQ'. He, it would appear, considers the sending of a 'DB' of more importance than the running of a class 'B'. But, after all, he too desires to get things done, and, like his signalman critic, is impatient of delay.

Do I like my job? Well, it is certainly interesting and at times exciting. Best of all, it is unique; there is no other job like it. But, to the levers and a medley of bells. My time is up, and there goes that telegraph instrument.

Scaled Down

One feature of the old railway companies was that they set much store on self improvement for their employees and in training. The LMS was to the fore in this setting up its own School of Transport, at Derby, but its main competitor had a young signalman. Strang Watson, a signalman at Falahill, Midlothian, whose ideas for a 'practical model railway' were very much in the same vein as those applied by the LMS and later British Railways at their training schools. This piece comes from the *North Eastern & Scottish Magazine*.

I have always had a longing to possess a model railway, which was not merely a railway where one exhibited a model train and showed a few signals dotted about the line to make it look the correct thing, but a railway that would be in every sense of the word a real working model, correct in every detail. The photographs reproduced herewith will give readers a very good idea of the extensiveness of my line, necessary in fact to work out and perform the many evolutions which take place in real practice. The railway at the time of writing is in no way yet complete, and therefore I cannot give any special programme of working, but no doubt a short chat about the system and its rolling stock will be interesting to readers. The whole of this system is correctly signalled and interlocked. The number of signal frames is thirteen, ranging from thirteen levers to the largest frame, which has fifty-five levers; cross-overs and sidings are fitted with working ground discs, all interlocked to the signal frame. The different sections are set out, and diagrams are provided with instructions for working.

I have a low level track running under the main track which I have named Queen Street [the LNER terminus in Glasgow] and King's Cross, the entire run from Queen Street to King's Cross being 295 feet. The higher level is reached by an incline which is 1 in 45, rather severe no doubt, but space prevented anything less. However, I can send a four-coach train up with comparative ease, and for heavier trains a banking engine is kept at the foot of the bank to assist these up to the top. Two turntables are provided, one being at Queen Street and the other at St Anne's Junction with accommodation for six engines. Working water columns are also set up at convenient parts of the system to allow engines to take in water. Both steam and clockwork locomotives are used, the steam locomotive being capable of a half-an-hour non-stop run. The clockwork engines are used mostly for dealing with suburban and goods traffic. The rolling stock on my line comprises:

Locomotives:
   One 4-6-0 *Sir Sam Fay*, GCR Section
   One 2-6-0 steam, GNR Section
   Two 0-6-2 clockwork tank, GNR Section
   Three 0-4-0 clockwork shunting tank, LNER Section
   One 4-6-0 steam, LNER Section
   One 4-4-2 clockwork tank, LNER Section

All the engines are painted in LNER colours.

Coaching Stock includes:
  Eight bogie passenger coaches
  One twelve-wheel dining car
  Two four-wheel bogie Post Office vans (working models)
  Four four-wheel bogie composite coaches
  Two four-wheel bogies passenger brake vans

Goods Stock:
  Six brake vans
  Eleven covered goods vans
  Twenty-four open trucks
  Six cattle wagons
  Three horse boxes
  Three petroleum wagons
  Two 30-ton bogie trucks
  One 30-ton NER high-capacity covered van

Accessories, such as goods depot, cattle pens, loading gauges, tail lamps, shunters' poles, &c., are also used.

There are five lever frames in use on the high section, four of which are completed, and situated thus:

St Anne's Box . . . . 24 lever frame.
St Anne's West 13   ''
Crawford Junctn 19   ''
Crawford East Box 13   ''

Eighty-four signals have already been fitted, nineteen ground discs, and thirty-three points. When finally completed, the total number of levers used for the system will be 372. The whole of the track is built on shelving, supported by stout trestles. Steel rail correct bull head section is used with cast chairs laid on hard wood sleepers to a gauge of 1¾ inch and ballasted with small granite chips which give a very realistic appearance. Up to the time of writing over 970 feet of track has been laid. The sleepers are placed 2-inch apart, and thirty-six chairs to the yard are used, the total number of chairs being 11,579. All sidings are finished off with rail-built buffer stops. Hydraulic buffer stops are used in the stations, The whole of the work is being constructed for me by that well-known firm, Messrs Bassett-Lowke, of Northampton, to my own ideas, and when completed will, I hope, be the means of working out railway problems, with all its intricacies in signalling and marshalling of trains. I extend a cordial welcome to any reader interested to view my railway if he will apply to me through the post so that I may make suitable appointment for doing so.

One can only assume that this man not only had a house with large rooms, but some considerable means of income at his disposal. Certainly not the ordinary run of railway signalmen of the day.

Chapter 14

Marketing the Railway

The railways were conscious of the need to market themselves, and often did so jointly, sometimes with all four companies putting their initials to advertisements for such matters as 'luggage in advance'* or taking one's dog by train, and sometimes using the collective title of the 'British Railways', especially for overseas marketing with offices opened jointly in Paris and New York. Even before grouping, there was much collaboration, with the East Coast Group of Companies and the West Coast Group created to advertise their competing services, but with the former including three large companies and the latter two.

The railways didn't simply sell to overseas customers, they also went on fact finding trips, looking for and taking on new ideas.

At home, there were competitions for the best chalked blackboards at stations advertising cheap day returns and excursions. Railway employees were encouraged to 'tell their friends' about improvements in services or special offers.

Even Sir Herbert Walker, the Southern Railway's far-sighted and imaginative general manager, was not above putting promotional stickers on letters he wrote in reply to correspondence from the public. On opening the letter, the correspondent would find that it had a green and yellow sticker showing a train headed by a King Arthur-class locomotive and the legend, 'The Sun Shines Most On The Southern Coast', or an orange and green sticker showing an electric multiple unit and the slogan, 'Live in Kent or Surrey and Keep Well'. The actual

---

* This was a wonderful system that many passengers would appreciate today. It could mean one's heavy luggage being collected from one's home and delivered to the holiday destination address, and vice versa for the return journey. Or it could be from one's local station to the destination station, and again vice versa for the homeward journey. One could even have it collected from the house and then pick it up at the destination station – the variations were considerable. There was, of course, a charge, depending on the level of service wanted.

advertising as the electric network expanded was 'Live in Kent and Be Content', or 'Live in Surrey, Far from Worry', so not surprisingly there was no such slogan for Sussex! But, of course, we are more concerned with the steam age.

Hard Times

No one should be in any doubt that the railways between the wars struggled with difficult economic conditions, made worse by the impact of the General Strike in 1926 and the much longer running strike by coal miners that prompted it. The dispute saw many export markets for coal lost altogether, which impacted on the traffic available to the railways.

Anxious to stimulate passenger traffic, at Christmas in 1932, the companies experimented with 'penny-a-mile' fares. These were a success and in the hope of stimulating traffic and, of course, revenue, they were re-launched in April 1933 for that year's holiday season. Eventually all of the 'Big Four' companies participated in this scheme. *The Great Western Railway Magazine* told its readers about it in an editorial.

> To encourage railway travel during the summer months, there will be an attractive reduction in fares. What will be known as 'Summer Tickets' will be issued for use from the beginning of May to the end of September. These bookings, both first and third class, will be given *on every day of the week between any pair of stations on the Great Western Railway, subject to a minimum fare of 2/6 third class and 4/- first class, and will be available by all trains without exception, and with availability for return either on the same day or any subsequent day up to one calendar month.*
>
> The fares will be based on the ordinary single fare and one-third for the return journey – equal to one penny per mile.

On the same page the company showed its financial results for the four weeks to 12 March 1933 compared with those for the same period in 1932, with passenger receipts down by 4 per cent, and these were the least badly affected of any part of the company's traffic, with those for general merchandise down by more than 10 per cent while coal and coke traffic was down by around 6 per cent. What is noticeable is that the conditions for using the tickets were simple, with no complicated conditions. The ticket holders were also entitled to reserve seats on the trains for the fee of a shilling each way, and the fact that any train could be used also meant that onboard refreshment facilities such as the dining cars could be used.

For the purpose of comparison, a penny-a-mile in 1933 would be equivalent to 17.5p a mile today. That would make it more expensive than current special offers booked on the Internet, but as the tickets could be used on any train, it would be far cheaper than the standard return fares of today which are well in excess of 30p per mile.

This was not the only initiative at this time. The *Southern Railway Magazine* for February 1931 had a front cover photograph showing a dog having his season ticket inspected, with a caption saying that season tickets for dogs 'should prove very popular'.

Launching the 'Golden Arrow'

The most important steam train for the management of the Southern Railway was the all-Pullman 'Golden Arrow', the first of two trains introduced between the wars to counter growing air competition. It was not the only interesting train on the Southern, and the 'Atlantic Coast Express', known to railwaymen as the 'ACE', had the distinction of being one of the trains to divide into the most portions, if not the most, as it attempted to serve the holiday resorts of North Devon and North Cornwall, with sometimes a resort receiving just a single composite carriage which reached its final destination attached to the local branch train.

Even more interesting was the train that many people refuse to believe ever existed, the 'Night Ferry', which used scaled down *Wagons Lits* sleeping cars to provide a through service from London Victoria to Paris, with the carriages shunted onto a train ferry for the overnight crossing from Dover to Dunkirk. Contemporary accounts say that the shunting was conducted with commendable quietness, but passengers were then awakened by the noise of the carriages being shackled to the deck, and then they were locked inside for the crossing. Compare this with modern cross-channel ferries which do not allow access to the vehicle deck during the passage.

First, however, the old London & South Western had neither named locomotives nor its trains, and although by now an old LSWR man himself, Walker was persuaded by his newly appointed press officer

John Elliott, to do both. In Elliott's autobiography, *On and Off the Rails*, he recalls the policy change.

> I ... proposed that we should give names to our express engines. Walker was doubtful at first but I pointed out that railways all over the world had found that people liked engines which had names. There was, I said, a real element of goodwill in this to be had at little cost. He asked me what names I had in mind. I gave him a sheet of paper with the names of King Arthur's knights from Malory's *Morte d'Arthur*, since the Southern Railway's North Cornwall line ran near Tintagel and I felt sure we could cash in on the old legend. The engines so named would be known as the 'King Arthur' class. Walker agreed, but said that he would have to consult the Locomotive Committee of the Board first. A few days later he told me I could go ahead and fix up the details with Maunsell, Chief Mechanical Engineer. To my surprise Maunsell liked the idea and said he would have a nameplate made up, and if I liked it could be fixed over the splashers of one of the passenger 4-6-0s ... However, it was not all plain sailing because ASLEF, the enginemen's union, objected to the name *Joyous Gard* and rang up the Secretary, asking plaintively, 'What about the bleedin' driver?' At that, Sir Charles Morgan, a former Chief Engineer of the LBSCR, and a director of the Southern Railway, was upset by *Morgan le Fay*!

Next came the naming of trains. After Elliott was involved with the naming of the 'Atlantic Coast Express', next came the 'Golden Arrow', but this was the idea of Sir David Dalziel, Chairman of the International Sleeping Car Company, who decided to give the name to the 11.00am 'Continental' from Victoria, and allowed himself to be persuaded by Walker that it should be first-class only. In fact, in the late 1930s, the passengers boarding at Victoria were said to look like a page from *Who's Who*. The French Nord Railway provided a matching train, and in between the Southern had all first-class steamer, *Canterbury*, dedicated to the service. This was extravagant, bearing in mind that modern short sea crossing ferries would normally make four return crossings daily and not just the one! Nevertheless, utilisation of equipment was far less at the time than today. Elliott again, on the inauguration.

I well remember the inauguration party on the day of the initial run to Paris on 15 May 1929. Among the guests were Lord Churchill, Chairman of the Great Western – though why he was there I don't know – and many others well known on both sides of the Channel, particularly Javary, Director-General of the Nord Railway of France and Walker's friend, and Baron Snoy, Director-General of the Wagons Lits. The Prefect of the Department, the Inspectors of Customs and the Chief of Police were waiting for us as we descended on Calais in the new cross-Channel ship *Canterbury*, which had been specially designed and built for the service by Denny of Dumbarton, builders of all SR cross-Channel ships for many years.

Canvassing for Goods Traffic

The team of men who sought goods traffic for the railways were sometimes known as 'canvassers', although the *Great Western Railway Magazine* described them as 'outdoor representatives'. This was partly because their work did not always involve visits to the offices of business undertakings, but could involve work at markets, for example.

The extent of railway involvement in goods transport at the time is hard for many to appreciate today. Household removals often involved railways, especially once the use of containers became more widespread so that not only was the time taken to transfer goods from lorry to railway wagon, and then back again at the other end of the journey, much reduced, but the safety of the contents was also enhanced. Entire farms would be moved by railway, with an entire train used if necessary. When the circus moved, it went by train, and the railways even had special wagons to accommodate elephants! The elephants would parade between the circus grounds and the railway station, helping to publicise the attraction.

Instead of an account of his day's work, we have abstracts from a paper presented to the Institute of Transport, predecessor of the current Chartered Institute of Transport and Logistics, in late 1930, on the work of the outdoor representative on the GWR.

What should be the equipment of a railway representative? Such qualities as courtesy and tact are the first essentials, but a good salesman should, by his personality, zeal, and belief in his job, endeavour to inspire the confidence of a prospective customer, and when once this is obtained, care must be taken not to lose it.

A representative should be adaptable, and quick to sense the atmosphere at an interview. A busy trader appreciates a business-like call, whereas it may happen that another trader has a few minutes to spare, and would enjoy a chat; in either case the wishes of a prospective customer should be met.

Interviewing traders, commission agents, etc., on markets is a different proposition from visiting offices, and opportunities must be sought and taken, in order to avoid incurring displeasure by interrupting buying and selling. This may appear to involve a waste of time, but the customer usually notices a representative waiting, and gives him a chance as soon as possible. One must, of course, be alert on this kind of canvassing, otherwise another transport representative may get there first.

It is unwise to make all sorts of rash promises which cannot be fulfilled; that is a sure way of losing confidence. An undertaking to do the utmost, with subsequent proof that you have done so, often brings good results.

A representative may be considered to be always on duty, and he should get to know his company's customers better by culti-vating the social side after usual business hours; incidentally, he will this make some very good friends. He should also be ever ready to do a little personal service.

In districts served by the Great Western Railway, the com-pany's own stations, trains, delivery vehicles, etc., are advertise-ments, but on foreign territory representatives should remember that they represent a personal advertisement for their company, and endeavour to live up to that responsibility.

Representatives of the company ought to have good all-round railway experience, as some surprising questions are put to them, and it is unfortunate if the representative shows a lack of knowledge.

On our own line, firms can be helped by the quick supply of special vehicles, and various other forms of attention at stations, but in outlying districts we have to rely on personal efforts, and to some extent on other companies. Especially must we depend on good transits, as quick delivery is the best advertisement for any company, and the greatest aid to canvassers ... I wonder if it occurs to a porter or a shunter, for instance, that a little extra effort to ensure the safe transhipment of a package, or the forwarding of a truck, makes a vital difference to the company and also to his own welfare, to say nothing about the representative who has probably walked miles (possibly in the rain) to secure the traffic, and who in the case of delay, will have to cover the ground again and explain, as best possible, the long transit, probably to be told that in future lots will be sent by road.

This was before the LMS, LNER and GWR agreed to combine their efforts in selling their goods services and coordinated collections and deliveries in order to cut costs and avoid overlap and duplication. The SR was not a party to this agreement because it was the least dependent on goods traffic, and also had minimal overlap with other companies. In London, coordination did not work so well and was not so necessary as the higher density of business houses and the availability of termini for each of the four grouped companies made separate arrangements worthwhile.

The Importance of Livery

Transport operators talk about livery, or sometimes colour schemes and few at the time would have known what is meant today by corporate identity. Nevertheless, this is an important factor ensuring that a company stands out from others and in transport it can be important in ensuring that the passenger identifies the right operator. Through trains from other companies did run over the Southern, and at stations such as Exeter St David's, Weymouth and Reading, the company's trains rubbed shoulders with those of the Great Western Railway at all times of the day. That apart, a good clean colour scheme plays its part in encouraging customers to think that the company has some pride and can assure them that its rolling stock has been properly looked after.

In 1936, the hotel proprietors on the Isle of Wight had suffered a poor season and the Southern's General Manager, Sir Herbert Walker, took a small team of his managers to investigate. The SR operated the entire railway network on the island, where three small companies had been absorbed on grouping after an earlier effort to 'group' themselves, while the company operated all but one of the ferry services to the island and traffic to and from the island used its services from

Waterloo and Victoria to Portsmouth Harbour, and from Waterloo to Southampton and Lymington Pier. Between 1913 and 1936, the summer Saturday service on the busiest of the Isle of Wight lines, that from Ryde to Sandown, Shanklin and Ventnor, had almost trebled, up from thirteen trains a day to thirty-eight.

In Charles Klapper's biographical account of Sir Herbert Walker's work on the SR, one Roger Arnold tells of one of Walker's visits to the island when the subject of colour schemes came up. Arnold was one of two young aides who accompanied the party, just in case any 'running' had to be done.

> All the way down to Portsmouth and across on the paddle steamer *Duchess of Norfolk*, and then on the train to Sandown, a triangular conversation went on while three of the four eminent men in the compartment argued about the effect of rolling stock colour on passenger bookings. Cox wanted a lovely green with golden lining; Bushrod thought green all over would be attractive; Maunsell plumped for dark unlined grey, with large white numerals on the tenders of engines – just the finish he had produced for his first 2-6-0 under the stress of war in 1917. Sir Herbert took no part but evidently thought a lot about colour schemes. After the gloomy news of the hotel industry was confirmed by actual observation and Sir Herbert had insisted on paying for the lunches of the two aides, who had not the opportunity of Lucullian lunches in the ordinary way, Sir Herbert went across to an optician's shop, where reels of spectacle thread were displayed in the window. He dashed in, emerged quickly with a length of green cord, produced small scissors, and cut off a piece for each of the officers. He still had an abundant part of the reel. 'Now, argument shall cease; that will be the colour Southern engines and coaches shall be painted in future. This reel shall remain in my office safe as the standard to which reference shall be made.' When Oliver Bulleid became responsible for the painting of Southern locomotives and coaches the choice of malachite green was thus made inevitable by a general manager who had retired a fortnight before Bulleid's appointment began.

Today, much money would have been spent on corporate identity consultants, but Walker was known for always seeking value for money. He took up office with the LSWR while the rebuilding of

Waterloo station was just starting, replacing with a single integrated structure four different buildings that had been built as traffic increased. The design was for a single all-over canopy, but he exempted the 'Windsor lines' part of the station which was still new, and had its own glass canopy, albeit lower than that proposed for the terminus as a whole, because of the savings that could be made. Those who knew Waterloo before the Eurostar platforms were built, can recall that his economy had no serious effect on the attractiveness or efficiency of the terminus as a whole.

Chapter 15

Wartime – In a Target Area

The railways had contributed much to Allied victory during the First World War, not simply providing the services that the armed forces and industry needed, but also losing men, often valuable skilled workers, to the war effort, seeing locomotives and rolling stock taken overseas, and the railway workshops concentrating on war work rather than the needs of the railways. A Railways Executive Committee was formed and, as mentioned earlier, this was under the *de facto* chairmanship of Herbert Walker, General Manager of the London & South Western Railway, for which he was knighted.

The same arrangement was introduced for control of the railways during the Second World War, albeit on far less attractive financial terms as compensation for state control was based on the average of three years before the outbreak of war, and the years between the wars had not been good for the railways, in contrast to the prosperity enjoyed by most, but not all, companies in the run up to the First World War.

Wartime conditions placed a great strain on the railways and railway workers as well as passengers who had to face lengthened trains, more stops, longer journeys, overcrowding and the virtual disappearance of train catering and such amenities as sleeping cars, which were generally reserved for senior personnel in the armed forces and for officials, while on suburban services first-class accommodation 'disappeared' in the sense that it was available to everyone and the first-class signs in windows and one doors removed. Yet, many of the problems and incidents of the peacetime railway continued, as this tale from Gerard Fiennes' *I Tried to Run a Railway* reveals.

Accident in Wartime

The first accident that Fiennes encountered was to a partly fitted goods train during the blackout after he had been posted to Scotland. The first thirteen wagons of the train were fitted with the vacuum brake, while the remainder only had handbrakes that could be applied and released by shunters whilst these wagons were moving slowly, except for the guard's van, which also had manual braking. The train came to a stand in the Haymarket tunnel on the up line, the line leading to Waverley, and the driver immediately assumed a vacuum failure and sent his fireman back to check. After a while, he returned saying that he couldn't find a problem. The driver also got down from the engine and the two of them went back along the train, and at the end of the fitted section they heard the hiss of drawn air. The driver watched while the fireman reset the rear pipe on the plug and then rejoin him. They started to walk back to the locomotive.

> Choo ... choo ... choo ... choo ... choo choo choo. She was away. No one on the footplate. The driver clawed his way to the nearest telephone on a signal post. He rang Waverley signalbox. The signalman looked at his diagram. The line to Portobello and the south was full of trains. The line to Granton Docks was clear. He set the road for Granton. He phoned the station staff to warn the guard.
>
> The train emerged from the tunnel at maybe 15 mph. By the time the brake emerged she was doing 20 mph. The guard was on the rear platform, leaning on the rail, drawing at an empty pipe upside down. The inspectors and porters shouted and waved their hats and flung their arms to heaven. The guard waved back. He thought they were wishing him many happy returns of his birthday, which it was. He realised that something was wrong when he recognised the steep down gradient on the Granton branch. The train was then doing 50 mph. He chose a grassy bank and alighted. He didn't even break his pipe. We spent four days at Granton picking up the mess.

Even in wartime there had to be an inquiry. Clearly the driver was at fault alighting from the locomotive leaving the regulator wide open, and he should also have ensured the locomotive was braked as well. The fireman had been careless missing the faulty vacuum connection the first time.

Blitzed at Cannon Street

Working on the railway in wartime was no easy task. During the First World War, railway travel had been the safest mode of transport;

during the Second World War, it became the most dangerous as the men, fuel and materials being moved by the railways made them prime targets. It was not necessary either for a railway line to be bombed, as an enterprising fighter pilot could be just as effective in putting a steam locomotive out of service as a bomber crew, with the difference that the former was in and out quickly, away before anti-aircraft gunners could get into their stride. It wasn't necessary to blow the wheels off a steam locomotive or put it into the middle of a large crater as a boiler riddled with bullets, or even better, blasted apart by cannon shell, was of no use and would take some considerable time to repair, requiring highly skilled manpower and scarce raw materials, including non-ferrous metals.

None of this, of course, can truly give a real impression of what it must have been like operating a railway in the blackout, or of the problems of individual railwaymen, and women, having to report for work after a broken night's sleep in a crowded air raid shelter, or of coming off a night shift in the morning to find that their home no longer existed, and perhaps face the loss of family members and neighbours as well. The efficient working of a railway required skill and experience, but under wartime conditions most adults had to be available for either the armed forces or prepared to be directed to essential war work, and as skilled men volunteered or were conscripted into the armed forces, many of their places were taken by women.

The final raid of the 'Blitz' was on the night of 10/11 May 1941, and was one of the worst. Waterloo was damaged by at least fifty-one high explosive bombs, incendiaries and parachute mines, while the incendiaries started a major fire after they penetrated into a spirits store in the arches beneath the terminus. In fact one unexploded 2,000-lb bomb was not discovered until work started on an adjoining office building in 1959. Cannon Street also suffered from bombs and incendiaries, and the locomotive that tried to rescue a van train by pulling it out from under the blazing roof onto the bridge was itself struck by a bomb. Holborn Viaduct was gutted by fires started by incendiary bombs and could not be used until 1 June. At Elephant & Castle, the island platform and up local platforms were burnt out, and a temporary up main platform had to be provided before it could re-open on 1 September. In *War on the Line*, published by the Southern Railway in 1946, Driver L. Stainer, of Bricklayers' Arms, recalled that night.

We stopped the engine at Borough Market and the fireman put out incendiaries. On arriving at Cannon Street, Platform 6, bombs began to drop, then the aspect signal lights all went out, and then some bombs dropped outside the station, bringing clouds of dust.

A fire had then started at the side of the station, and it rained bombs and there seemed to be no stopping. The fires were then like huge torches and there were thousands of sparks.

The smoke from the fires blacked out the moon, and fires seemed to be everywhere, and then the station roof caught alight.

To save the trains catching fire, two engines coupled together, No. 934 and 1541, pulled out of Platform 8 on to the bridge. We stopped 20 yards ahead of the other train, and then, after about ten minutes we ducked down on the footplate. We counted three bombs, the last one was terrific and very close. There was a terrific explosion and our engine seemed to roll; at first we thought our train had been hit. The debris flew in all directions – we were very lucky. My fireman said at the time, 'Look out – we are going in the drink', and I said, 'I thought my back week had come.'

We looked round, and found that the bomb had made a direct hit on the boiler of No. 934 engine, and it had also blasted our train, and turned part of the train over on its side.

My fireman and myself went to see where the driver and fireman were, and I am pleased to say that they had got off the engine in time.

Then, looking around, we found our train had caught fire, and the fireman with buckets of water tried to put same out, but it was impossible as a strong wind was blowing up the Thames, and the fire got the master.

I uncoupled my engine from the train, and drew back about 2 yards, and scoured the engine, and then crossed to the west of the bridge until dawn, watching the fires. It was just like as if Hell had been let loose.

Fortunately, no one was injured and Driver Stainer paid tribute to the coolness of the station staff at Cannon Street.

In Yorkshire

Alone amongst Britain's railways, the LNER introduced its own silver 'LNER Medal' for acts of heroism during wartime. The most notable of these was on the night of 2 June 1944, when the driver and fireman of a trainload of bombs on fire at Soham in Cambridgeshire uncoupled the blazing wagons and took them away from the town before they exploded, killing Fireman Nightall and seriously injuring Driver Gimbert. Both men received the George Cross as well. Had the blazing wagons exploded in the town the place would have been flattened, for as it was the explosion left a crater 66 feet in diameter and 15 feet deep, damaging 700 houses in Soham and wrecked the signal box and station master's house.

Further north, but still on the LNER, N. Dixon was by now an established fireman who was allowed to drive as a relief when a rostered driver was absent, but he was confined to pilot locomotives.

He had had a difficult first year of war, being involved in two accidents whilst firing, the second of which saw his locomotive run into the wreckage of a fish train that had just crashed. Although badly shaken and bruised, he ran to the signalbox to ensure that no further trains ran into the wreckage, finding the signalman in a state as he had seen the accident and expected Dixon's train to run into the signalbox. Dixon then returned to his train and then had to walk through the passenger carriages to see if there were any injuries. Fortunately there weren't. With his driver, Dixon had then to douse the fire of his locomotive, which had been badly damaged and risked exploding.

A sign of the times was that despite their ordeal and bad bruising, no one asked Dixon or his driver if they were fit for duty, and both reported as usual the following morning. Dixon claimed that after such an experience he wanted to back to work and, if he stayed off, he 'might be afraid to go on passenger work again'.

I moved into another house in 1940 and had only been in this one six weeks when in an air raid the front door was blown in and all the windows blown out. This was quite an experience as we were in the house at the time; my wife was not alone in thinking the end of the world had come! It was tragic working a train to say Doncaster or Leeds at night and on working the return trip, getting near Hull, one could see the city burning and wondered if your house would still be standing and the family safe. Working on the docks meant you were exposed to danger because they were the main target of the German bombers. I have had to dash for shelter many a time when bombs were falling and had near escapes several times. Going to work through the streets after a bad raid was a harrowing experience seeing houses and shops flattened, and people's furniture strewn all over the street.

Such problems were part and parcel of wartime life on the railways, with at least one accident occurring after a driver had been bombed out of his home shortly before, and in another case a driver was thought to have been exhausted through lack of sleep.

Chapter 16
Running a Railway

Most of the interest and attention in this book centres around the work that the old-time railwayman did, but running any transport undertaking is different from running any other kind of business, and not just because it is more interesting and the enthusiasm it engenders is shared by many of those 'on the inside'. It is often pointed out that the most perishable commodity in the world is the seat on a train (or any other mode of transport, and it applies to freight space as well) that is departing. Unlike the butcher, the baker or the candlestick maker, there is no further chance to sell it. There is another difference. Planned time off can easily be lost if a disaster occurs and management cannot walk away in such a situation. Remedial action must be taken, ensuring all that can be is done for the survivors and that the relatives of those killed or injured, many of whom may be employees, are notified and attention given to their needs. At the same time, action has to be taken to minimise disruption and get services back to schedule. Even while this is happening, there will also be the need to assist the authorities in their investigation of the accident. In countries that are well run, the investigators will release any information that they feel may prevent a repeat of the accident as soon as they have it, even before the final report is ready, and here again action has to be taken by the management of a transport undertaking to ensure that steps are taken immediately.

As we have seen, the age of the steam railway was very different from today. Management differed as well. Obviously there were no computers, no Internet or 'intranet' or mobile phones, but there were also precious few management books or courses on management. Training was different, and few organisations had management training schemes. What happened was that someone in authority would settle upon an individual who seemed to possess the right qualities, and this person would serve in effect an apprenticeship, being trained by example. Much of the daily task would consist on the railways of the prospective manager acting as a 'runner', literally being a messenger and at the same time being able to gather the threads of what was happening.

When the readers of the magazine *Modern Railways* were polled to see who deserved the title of the best railwayman of all time the clear favourite was one Sir Herbert Ashcombe Walker, who came to fame as the last general manager of the London & South Western Railway and the first of the Southern Railway on grouping in 1923. He was originally destined to be a doctor, his family circumstances brought his training to an early end and at the age of seventeen years he found himself working for the Superintendent of the Line at the London & North Western Railway's London terminus at Euston. While he advanced within the LNWR, and frequently represented the company at major inquiries, he was not appreciated by them and it was unlikely that he would have risen to the top of the LNWR and its successor, the LMS. Instead, he was approached by the London & South Western Railway in 1912, and became its last general manager and the first general manager of the Southern Railway. His role as *de facto* chairman of the Railway Executive Committee during the First World War, for which he received his knighthood, showed that the LSWR had made the right choice.

Walker had a remarkable ability to remember facts and figures, and the names, including Christian names, of the people whom he met; and was numerate. His memory extended to such matters as track layouts, signalling circuits, the capacities of sidings and even the locking boxes in signal boxes in his territory.

In his book, *Sir Herbert Walker's Southern Railway*, Charles Klapper relates an event from the General Strike of 1926.

During the General Strike of 1926 he walked into 'A' box at Waterloo, where Leslie Harrington, one of his aides, was helping to hold the fort. Greeting the inspector in charge by name, he said 'Getting on all right?' to Harrington and the inspector. 'What have you got ready to start?' On being told, Walker said, 'Would you like me to set the road for it?' And without hesitation he went to the block instrument to obtain 'Line clear' from Vauxhall, then to the frame to pull the point levers, and on receiving the 'Ready to start' indication from the platform, he went to pull off the starting signal. With 'That all right?' to the inspector, he then left to give inspiration somewhere else.

One can't imagine this happening today, sadly.

Managing Grouping

Yet another amongst the greatest railwaymen was Sir Felix Pole of the Great Western Railway, who joined the company in 1891 and was appointed general manager in 1921, which meant that an important task was preparing the company for grouping in 1923. His experience also included the final conversion of the GWR from broad gauge to standard gauge in 1894. He left the railways in 1929 to move into manufacturing, but when his biography, *J.C. Felix Pole – His Book*, was published privately in 1954 (and later published publicly), most of it dealt with his time on the railways; a good example of what one Scottish engineer described as 'the particular "go"' of the transport story.

He had this to say about grouping.

The problem of welding together the lines amalgamated with or absorbed by the Great Western proceeded by stages. Of course, the various boards of directors (other than that of the Great Western), general managers, secretaries and other chief officers disappeared, but many officers of constituents companies were given official posts with the new Great Western ...

Many officers, however, retired, and this was easy to arrange because the Railways Act had laid down a scale of compensation which was certainly generous, but quite justifiable in view of the considerable economies that were affected. Of course, much expenditure was involved in constructing new or re-arranging existing lines in order to facilitate railway and dock working. The officers of the various departments were asked to prepare schemes and were told that there would be no delay in obtaining the approval of the Board of Directors. Before long, the advantages of the increased facilities became apparent, although some of the schemes were found to be on unduly generous lines and had to be curtailed.

It must not be supposed that officers of lines which had been keen rivals, at once settled down in brotherly cooperation. Indeed, there were from time to time complaints that the railway and dock departments were not working harmoniously together. In the early part of 1926, I personally went to Cardiff with other officers to make an investigation. All the local officers concerned were present and I came to the conclusion that two of them – former rivals – could remove all difficulties provided that they had the will to do so. After the meeting I had a little talk with them and told them I felt sure they held the key of the situation, and that as soon as I was satisfied that coal trains were being worked freely from pit to port they should each receive a cheque for a generous amount. Needless to say, the cheques were soon called from and there was no more complaint that collieries were being stopped because loaded wagons had not been removed or because empties had not been supplied.

The Way In

Gerard Fiennes lost his job as general manager of the Eastern Region of British Railways in 1967 for writing a book, *I Tried to Run a Railway*. No doubt it was wrong of him to do so whilst in the employment of BR, but his book remains a 'must read' for anyone with an interest in railways, and of what worked and what didn't. His description of the Beeching years is especially enlightening because the good Doctor Beeching had many brilliant ideas, but is remembered for the closures of stations and lines, not all of them branches, carried out in his name. In fact his methodology was wrong, and in particular failed to give resort stations any recognition for the revenue they generated because the return tickets had, of course, been sold at other stations. He also failed to appreciate the scope for running many branch lines more cheaply.

In 1930, Fiennes' career started on the old LNER, although he also spent some time on BR's Western Region. He describes his old company's entry procedure at the start of the book.

The LNER's system for training traffic apprentices was run pretty well single-handed by the Assistant General Manager, Robert Bell. He selected a few men from the salaried staff, ostensibly by competitive examination; handpicked a few more direct from the minor public and grammar schools; and got the remainder via the appointments boards at the universities.

He had principles. One of them was no nepotism. Few sons, nephews or cousins of the directors came on to the LNER. If one did, his life was especially difficult. I can't remember one lasting the course, let alone rising in the service. Secondly, the LNER was poor but honest. Traffic apprentices were the same. He said to me in his slow, dry Scots, 'You may expect, if you are successful, to become a district officer at a salary of £800 a year.' Ten years later he appointed E.J. Stephens to District Superintendent, Lincoln, at £700. We were certainly poorer. Thirdly, there was to be no skulking around within reach of home. Scotsmen and Geordies went to the Southern Area; Cockneys went to Scotland. Luckily mother was in Brittany and I drew the south. Fourthly, there must be no communication. Two traffic apprentices together is no traffic apprentice. Lastly the basic railway is what matters. Training was at stations, small and large, marshalling yards, loco-motive depots, control offices, offices for timing and diagram-ming, and for townsmen and claims.

We spoke to an officer perhaps ten times a year. We were taught our trade by the men who plied those trades. At the time I missed the point. I went slavishly on training as if it was a projection of school. I hadn't a clue of the pattern and purpose behind it all. I was, as Dillington House has so rightly said of traffic apprentices like me – 'a thrombosis: a bloody clot in the system'.

The training was thorough and did not neglect the basics. Fiennes found himself issuing tickets and doing the daily balance and pas-senger classification, monthly balance and returns, passengers and freight. He had to get eighty trusses of hay into a wagon, sheet and rope it properly, as well as knowing how to use a shunting pole and brake stick to apply the brakes on unfitted goods wagons. He also learnt a few unorthodox moves, such as rolling two milk churns at a time, until one day one of them rolled under an express, so that the air was full of whining metal, '... and later of whining rockets from district office ...'

In the next two-and-a-half years the programme took me to London, Manchester, Leeds, Southend and Parkeston [the main LNER ferry port for sailings to the Low Countries]. I went on learning by rote and not by understanding. Nevertheless, by this method examinations came easily to me. The last and crowning glory was the oral examination in rules and regulations in front of the Superintendent's Chief Signalling Inspector, Ricket. He grilled me for three hours. I was, I believe, word perfect ... I found out how little actual understanding I had when a year later I found myself putting in single line working in emergency between Whitemoor Junction and Coldham. But as always at Whitemoor there was somebody to tell the incompetent how to do it: in this case the signalman on duty, Bob Wright.

It was clearly not a glamorous job. Fiennes spent some days relaying track in the Woodhead tunnel, which runs under the Pennines and is on a rising gradient. He also experienced the tunnel from the footplate: '... grim moments on the footplates of up trains slipping in the tunnel in a smother of smoke and steam with the fireman and myself down on hands and knees in search of breath for long past eternity ...'. He built a brick arch in the firebox of a steam locomotive, which stood up for a few weeks, and worked inside the locomotives on tubes and fireboxes. This was not the sort of background one would expect for what might be considered an office job, but in fact traffic apprentices had to know how everything worked not only to command the respect of those beneath them, but also to stop them from making silly mistakes when they finally got to run a railway. Nevertheless, there is the feeling that while he became a railway jack of all trades, he could not but escape the criticism of being master of none! But then the individual trades were of themselves a career for many a railwayman.

Getting On at the Southern

In 1925, Sir Herbert Walker at the Southern Railway decided that the company needed to improve its relations with the press, and in a bold move he recruited John Elliott from the *Evening Standard*, then one of three London evening newspapers, to be his public relations and advertising officer. The appointment was a great success, apart from the story below about boosting off-peak traffic, and after five years it was felt that Elliott needed a more challenging role and he became the traffic manager's assistant for development, which at the time was the term used for marketing. He was not to know that he was being groomed for higher things, as he found out after a meeting in April 1933.

Early in April 1933, as I followed Bushrod and the other officers out of Cox's handsome room on the second floor at the end of his morning conference – an affair which I greatly enjoyed and listened to like a small boy trespassing into the sixth form – he called me back. 'Sit down for a moment,' he said. 'The Manager wants to see you about making a railwayman out of you. Don't ask questions. I am coming with you, so let's go now.'

Walker was standing by the fireplace. 'Good morning, Elliott,' he said, and then to Cox, 'Ask Gilbert to come in, too.' When we were seated round the fire Walker spoke again. 'We have been thinking for some time that there is not much more you can do where you are. It's time we put you out on the line. You have a lot to learn. Spend as much time outside as you can – go on inspections, get to know and understand the men, watch signalmen at work, until you have learnt the essentials of safe train operation. How do you feel about it all?' All I could say was that I felt very lucky and wanted to do nothing else. At that Walker said, 'Good. We are going to take a chance with you because we need young men to follow us.' My heart was pumping. 'Mr Cox has agreed that you shall have the title of Assistant Traffic Manager, to give you the necessary standing, but be careful not to throw your weight around; you will not be in a position to give orders to senior officers. We are putting you with them to learn, and if you make the most of your opportunities you could hope to get to the top one day.'

If anyone really walked on air, I did as I left the room with Szlumper. There was more to come as he beckoned me to join him. 'Now, J.B., it's in your own hands. I had to overcome the handicap of being the son of the Chief Civil Engineer (Albert Szlumper) and to mind my step when I was young. Listen, watch and always be where you are wanted, never where you are not. Get to know as many of the officers as you can, and don't get into arguments.' Then he treated me to a characteristic 'Who's Who' of the SR top brass and in his breezy style labelled them good chaps, fools and bloody fools. 'Come and see me whenever you like.' And with a firm handshake he sent me on my way.

I was thirty-five when Walker yanked me out of the selling side, and it turned out I had barely four and a half years in which to learn what made the railway tick. It involved endless travelling to all parts of the system, often by night, walking over important junctions and marshalling yards, into signal boxes, and attending traffic meetings at all the main railway centres. I also visited every city in Europe where the SR had its own offices or agents, and went twice to America. Two or three times a month I entered the forbidding portals of the Railway Clearing House in Eversholt Street, the ark of the railway covenant, where endless meetings were relentlessly turned into minutes.

This was typical of the grooming that a promising railway manager received, except that, and this is important, it was much accelerated.

Out on the Line (1)

Walker's demand that Elliott got out and about as much as possible stemmed from his own background and approach to management. When he arrived at the London & South Western he found that the company did not enjoy the highest reputation, and indeed many of his senior managers were obstructive. Given a month in which to produce a regular headway timetable for the Kingston roundabout services, which were amongst those hit by tramway electrification, Henry Holmes, the Superintendent of the Line, eventually came back with the claim that regular headways were for lesser railways and not for the LSWR.

Relations with Holmes were not improved by Walker travelling around the system more or less as a normal passenger, and finding that public disappointment with the company was often justified. Roger Arnold, who later served under Sir Herbert, tells the story of what happened when he arrived at Fareham from Southampton by train with his family, ready to catch the connecting service up the Meon Valley line.

We approached Fareham and just as our train came to a halt I espied another M7 4-4-0 tank heading a two-coach salmon and umber outfit standing in the bay. The guard was fingering his green flag ready to wave it just as we drew to a halt. But he did not! A stentorian roar from the footbridge came from a thunderclap of: 'Guard Grant. George Grant, hold that train!' ... a huge square shouldered man in a tweed overcoat, with pince-nez gold spectacles, came down and hurtled over the timber crossing from the island to the bay platform with the alacrity of a young athlete rather than a staid man in his forties. Once more his instinct for the detail paid off. With his furled umbrella like a foil at the ready he came up to the startled guard. 'Your name is George Grant? Mine is Herbert Ashcombe Walker. You were about to start this train before the passengers from the 5.50pm from Southampton could join, although this is the last train up the Meon Valley today!'

By this time the capless station master came running up to see what had caused the disturbance. Before he could collect his thoughts Walker was speaking again. 'Your name is Mr Peter Cooper; does this heinous thing take place every evening? If it does, let me assure you that it will not happen again without your coming to Waterloo.' A faint cheer from passengers within ear-shot. By then Walker had boarded the train and from a first-class compartment was asking Cooper if he could telephone Alton. 'Yes, sir.' 'Then tell Mr Smith that this train connects with the 8.20pm to Surbiton and Waterloo and if it does not do so then *he* can come to Waterloo and see me in the morning!'

The outcome of incidents such as this was that Walker wasted no time in tightening up the operating department, giving district super-intendents sole control in all matters other than accidents, rates and fares.

Out on the Line (2)

Elliott followed Walker's injunction to get out and about with the senior officers as much as possible. This also brought him into contact with senior officials from other railway companies, such as the Great Western, the Southern's neighbour, and the London Midland & Scottish, its partner in the Somerset & Dorset Joint Railway.

I remember particularly one occasion when the inspection saloon left for the West Country with Cox [Edwin Cox, the Traffic Manager] and several of his officers including myself on one side, and Nicholls, the well-liked, bearded GWR Superintendent of the Line on the other ... We arrived early next morning at Dorchester where it had been decided that the Southern should take over both stations, as we had the largest traffic. Led by Cox and

Nicholls, we tumbled out of the saloon to be met by the local stationmaster, the inevitable red rose in his buttonhole, with his staff of three lined up behind him. Cox, who, liked public speaking ... gave a dissertation on the new duties of the joint stationmaster acting for both companies and told him that everything depended on him and both staffs forgetting the past and thinking only of making the unified Southern and Great Western a useful part of the town ... Then it was Nicholls' turn and he was as brief as Cox had been long-winded. Shaking the stationmaster warmly by the hand, he said, 'Well, stationmaster, you know what you've got to do.' The answer came quickly: 'Yes sir, now we'll give these Great Western buggers 'ell!' So much for the joys of amalgamation.

Seeking Off-Peak Passengers

In a bid to boost off-peak traffic, John Elliott (later Sir John) embarked on an advertising programme, 'DOES YOUR WIFE KNOW?' to remind regular travellers that travelling between 9.00am and 5.00pm their return fare would be the same as the single fare. It worked. He then embarked on a campaign to encourage excursion traffic, including stopping trains at the main suburban stations to cut out the necessity to travel to the London termini, which had given coach operators the opportunity to take much of the excursion traffic from the suburbs. Some of the excursions were elaborate, including one to Portsmouth with a steamer connection to Ryde, a round-the-island coach tour to Yarmouth, followed by a steamer to Lymington, and then back onto the excursion train for the journey home. In his autobiography, *On and Off the Rails*, Elliott recalled the outcome.

Next summer ... I overstepped the mark and got the only severe criticism from [Sir Herbert] Walker that I can remember ... innovations had been a success, but at the end of the season I noticed with a sinking feeling that although the number of passengers carried was much higher, the total revenue was about the same as the previous summer.

Sure enough, I had a call from old Barfoot, Walker's personal secretary, saying the General Manager wanted to see me ... In due course I sat down at his big desk. Spread out on it were sheets from the Chief Accountant, with long columns of statistics showing passengers carried, mileage run by trains, steamers and motor coaches, and in the last column the next results, black or red. Walker looked up as I sat down and asked me whether I had seen the figures. I said I had … Walker said the cause of the trouble was that I didn't know, and ought to have known, and should have found out, what the extra mileage was costing. My blood ran cold.

Walker said, 'You have done well, but you must learn what we are here for. It is not just to please the public, but to enable us to pay ordinary dividends each year and so to be able to raise capital for further electrification … I am happy to carry more people for more money,' he said. 'I don't mind carrying fewer people for more money, but what you are asking me to do is carry more people for less money, and that's the way to go bankrupt. You will remember that, won't you?'

Punctuality

Punctuality has been a perennial problem on the railways, although it seems to have been better between the wars than post-war, when operations were affected not just by the backlog of repairs and maintenance accumulated during the war, but also by poor quality coal. One big difference between then and now was that trains were either 'on time' or 'late', whereas depending on the length of journey, today they are not regarded as late until at least five and often ten minutes have elapsed.

The General Strike of 1926 tore the timetables to tatters, and even once the railwaymen returned services took time to return to normal because of the shortage of coal as the miners, or 'colliers' in the language of the day, remained on strike for much longer. Nevertheless, even before this, as an editorial from the *North Eastern & Scottish Magazine* shows, 1926 began badly. Interesting, too, that this was the title of the magazine three years after grouping, although a sub-head had 'London & North Eastern Railway' in brackets and the grouped company's logo was also in evidence. The editorial was signed by Ralph Wedgwood, the chief general manager.

The year has opened with more than the usual allowance of weather troubles to try the patience of railwaymen, and of the operating staff in particular. We have had snow, floods and fog in abundance, and these in turn have reacted on our service, both for passenger and for goods traffic. The public always shows great indulgence to us when we are struggling with difficulties of this nature; nevertheless, complaints – some of them emphatically worded – are becoming increasingly frequent, and strong comment is made on the alleged unpunctuality of our passenger trains. Many of us have heard – and not once or twice only – that on certain sections of the line the public were able to set their clocks in the old days by the running of our trains, but we have now fallen very far from grace. I am afraid there is more than a grain of truth in the indictment.

It is difficult to test such criticisms thoroughly by comparison with our pre-war performance, but such comparisons as can be made do, unfortunately, support in regard to many of our services the reproach that is thrown up against us and the deterioration in these services is not confined to periods of fog or bad weather. We have no doubt many difficulties to encounter which are special to the present day, but I am convinced that a combined effort can do very much to remedy our present lapse from grace, and to re-establish us on that pinnacle of punctuality which every railway-man desires to occupy.

Punctuality is our first duty to the public, and a railway which is unpunctual, whatever its other virtues, can never win the esteem of the public which it serves. The secret of punctuality is team work and attention to detail – everyone can help by giving thought, and everyone can hinder, by taking things for granted. The stationmaster can help by seeing that his staff are on the spot before the arrival of the train and, after its arrival, by counting the seconds before it departs. The station staff and the guard can help by getting milk cans, luggage and parcels into, position before the train draws up, and, when the train is in, by attending first to the unloading and loading of the vans. The driver can help by making up lost time, whenever possible, between stations. The supervisory and timetable staff can help by maintaining a practical and workable schedule of trains. Every detail counts and unless they are all looked after time will inevitably be lost.

I believe every member of staff feels with me that the reproach of unpunctuality brings more discredit to a railway company than any other which can be levelled against it, and I am sure that every individual will redouble his efforts to secure a clean record for our company.

Of course, on reading this many will immediately say that safety is the most important virtue for any transport undertaking. However, punctuality is important along with running all advertised services.

On the 'Island'

Grouping brought together three small companies on the Isle of Wight which for the first time was a united network, but separated by the Solent from the mainland, it was also entire unto itself. The holiday traffic to and from the island was valuable to the Southern Railway, but it was also difficult to manage as the mainly single track network saw massive fluctuations in traffic between summer and winter, especially as the summer holiday season was far shorter and more intense than today. The largest of the pre-grouping railways on the island was the Isle of Wight Central Railway, which operated from Ryde to Newport and Cowes, and from Newport to Sandown and Shanklin with a branch to Ventnor West, while the smallest was the impoverished Freshwater, Yarmouth & Newport Railway, with just three engines at grouping, but until then had been worked by the IWCR. The busiest and most viable railway was the Isle of Wight Railway, with its solitary main line from Ryde to Ventnor, a distance of twelve and a half miles, with a branch from Brading to Bembridge and St Helens. The IWR served the main resorts and the main ferry port with the short crossing of three miles to Portsmouth, which was at the end of the most direct and shortest route from London, albeit not the fastest line and until electrification it had just four fast trains a day – after electrification on a summer Saturday it had as many in just one hour.

The problem was, of course, that in winter this was a quiet and underused railway, although especially in winter there were considerable shipments of household coal from Medina Wharf to the various station sidings occupied by coal merchants on the railway network. In summer, on the former IWR line, the train service was of London suburban intensity, but squeezed onto single track apart from the line from Ryde Pier Head to Ryde St John's, while slightly beyond to were operated by the IWCR and IWR as two adjoining single lines to Smallbrook Junction, where the Ventnor and Newport lines diverged.

Before grouping, the line as far as St John's had been owned jointly by the LSWR and the LBSCR.

A directors' inspection of the railway network on the island in August 1923 had shown serious problems, with dilapidated rolling stock, unsatisfactory stations and sheds and workshops in a poor condition with little protection for the men working in them. At the age of just twenty-eight, Alistair Macleod was appointed to run the railways on the island. He had been the junior of two assistants to the London East divisional locomotive running superintendent, and had been selected for being able to handle men, which was important for the 'hands on' role envisaged for him; and of being a railway enthusiast (something that was regarded as commendable at Waterloo, but suspect at King's Cross), as well as having flair and initiative. Initially he was responsible for locomotives and rolling stock, but was later also given responsibility for traffic.

He arrived on the island after a passing loop had been installed at Wroxall on the Ventnor line and doubling sanctioned of the line between Brading and Sandown, while the section between St John's Road and Smallbrook Junction was to be operated as a double track. Replacement locomotives and rolling stock were also being provided, albeit all with previous use on the mainland for until the end of steam, this remained a Victorian railway. Despite his wide-ranging responsibilities, his salary was, at £350, just below the £360 threshold for a first-class pass, and it took special permission for this to be granted, and even then, it was confined to the island lines.

Klapper records what life was like for the young MacLeod in *Sir Herbert Walker's Southern Railway*.

While the work of improvement was proceeding the island became the object of numerous excursions by officers – some managed casually such as a visit by E.C. Cox and his wife to Freshwater and across to Ryde, while on the way from London to Bournemouth, and others of a more official inspection character. On one of these, the lights in the coach in which the officers were travelling went out in Wroxall Tunnel, through the mistake of the electrical chargehand who had put in new batteries without discovering whether they were charged or not. At the culminating dinner nothing was said to spoil MacLeod's evening, but what a dressing down came from Maunsell in the morning on the lines of 'We are spending all this money in the Isle of Wight and all I get is a leg-pull about "fairy lights" in our coach.' Mrs Cox on one occasion raised hell about a bent penny not working the lavatory lock at Ryde Pier Head and 'where was the woman attendant for the ladies' Lavatory?' She got as good as she gave, it being pointed out that the tight budget for the island railways made no provision for such elaborations of staff. Cox saw to it that such an addition to the establishment was provided for in future.

All of this shows that Walker looked for opportunities to give young men their head, but did not allow them to get above themselves with such prestigious benefits as unlimited first-class travel. Macleod's own narrative appears in *Rails in the Isle of Wight*, which he wrote jointly with P.C. Allen.

> My predecessor met me and after a hurried lunch seemed anxious to leave as soon as possible for the mainland. We did, however, go down to the headquarters of the department which was at Ryde St John's Road, where I was warned that I must remember that I was an 'Overner' and not an 'Islander' and would have difficulty with the staff, some of whom were alleged to have Bolshevik tendencies. I was introduced to the locomotive carriage and wagon foremen and taken round the works. We then returned to Ryde Pier Head and I said goodbye and wished him luck. This was returned, and so I found myself in charge, with an independent command at the age of twenty-eight.
>
> Back then to St John's Road works for a look around, with an introduction to each member of the staff. I was a proper new boy and said I must go and get some 'digs'. The locomotive foreman gave me some addresses to go to but asked if I would first settle an urgent problem which had not been solved and was causing trouble. 'You see it's like this,' he said. 'The leading engine fitter caught an owl in the erecting shop this morning and won't let it go because he wants to sell it to a taxidermist for stuffing.' 'Why didn't you let it go?' I said. 'Well, you see how the fitter is a Bolshevik and very difficult,' he replied. 'Where's the bird?' I said. 'Oh, it's now in the oil stores,' he said. There was the unfortunate barn owl flopping about in one of the oil trays. The fitter was sent for and advised about cruelty to birds, also that the Southern Railway did not pay him to catch birds in the company's time and that he must try to clean off the oil with paraffin and put the bird

in a nearby wood. That settled that, and the owl was able to fly away, such was my introduction to the 'Garden Isle' … The running shed at Ryde St John's Road was deplorable. It consisted of a corrugated iron barn with a curved roof which just gave cover to four engines, standing over the inspection pits. There was a covered loading bank for a coal stage. This was all sandwiched into the goods yard, which made operations difficult.

The locomotive yard and running shed at Newport, however, were better and situated behind the goods yard, adjacent to the old IWCR workshops. The running shed had a louvred roof, which did allow the fumes and smoke from the engines to escape, unlike Ryde. Newport shed could also provide cover for at least eight engines over the pits; the coaling was carried out from an inadequate covered stage or out in the yard.

My first journey on the Newport–Freshwater line was eventful as some of the telegraph wires came adrift from the insulators and became wrapped round the 'Terrier's' chimney and this caused some delay in untangling the wires.

MacLeod soon came to the conclusion that under difficult conditions, the personnel were doing the best they could. Ryde St John's Road had other facilities, including the main repair works, housed in a large brick building with two bays, and attached to it were a number of sheds, some built of corrugated iron and some of wood, with a large water cistern that dated from 1870. Space was a problem as expansion was impossible because of the station on one side and the Small Brook on the other, which from time would burst its banks and flood both the station and the goods yard. Nevertheless, as he got to know the staff, he found them cooperative, and noticed no signs of Bolshevism. This was a time when the Russian revolution was still to the fore in many people's minds as just eleven years had elapsed. Today it is hard for us to realise what a jolt to the populations of the rest of Europe the event had been, especially as in post-war Germany and Austria attempts were made at revolution.

Scheduling

Preparing a railway timetable was a demanding task, but one through which most managers had to progress. They had to know the speed limits throughout the route as every inch of railway line has a speed limit, which varies, as well as the limitations of the motive power available; also, knowledge of such matters as stops and gradients, and conflicts with other trains at junctions. That this was far from a perfect art can be assessed from the fact that the London & South Western Railway, in pre-Herbert Walker days, would send three trains from Waterloo towards Exeter at ten-minute intervals – with the fastest train last.

Timetables were planned on graph paper and known as diagrams, hence a particular locomotive or multiple unit would be 'diagrammed' for certain workings. This is a 'train clerk's lament', compiled by one A.H. Smith, who worked in the District Superintendent's Office in Doncaster, and is from the *London & North Eastern Railway Magazine* – with apologies to Kipling:

If you can draw a 'graph'; put all your trains on
Employ your track to full capacity.
If you can still squeeze in a few excursions
Or book a new class 'B' to run at 'P'.
If you can shunt a train of sixty wagons
Into a siding made for forty-nine.
If you can send an up fast on its journey,
When, ahead, a down slow's backed across the line.

If you can get a class 'A' past a coal train
At a block post where no crossover exists.
If you can make a speed restriction 'twenty'
Whilst the engineer on 'only twelve' insists.
If you can push two Fliers through a junction
Within a minute, causing no delay;
If you can make six goods trains alterations
And not disturb your chart in any way.

If you can use one path, 'MO' for butter,
On 'W' and 'F' for frozen meat,
On 'Tu' and 'Th' run specials with bananas,
On 'SO' give the sporting fans a treat.
If you can solve these problems on a 'graph', Sir,
If you can show how such things might be done;
Well, really, you were born an ideal trains clerk,
And, what is more, you're wanted now, my son.

Bibliography

Allen, Cecil J., *Salute to the Southern*, Ian Allan, Shepperton, 1974.

Allen, Cecil J. *Titled Trains of Great Britain*, Ian Allan, London, 1946–67.

Allen, Cecil J. and Townroe, S.C., *The Bulleid Pacifics of the Southern Railway*, Ian Allan, Shepperton, 1951 & 1974.

Allen, P.C. and Macleod, A. B., *Rails in the Isle of Wight*, Allen & Unwin, London, 1967.

Barman, C., *The Great Western Railway's Last Look Forward*, David & Charles, Newton Abbot, 1972.

Beaumont, R., *The Railway King: A Biography of George Hudson railway pioneer and fraudster*; Review, London, 2002.

Bishop, D. and Davies, W.J., *Railways and War since 1917*, Blandford, London, 1974.

Bonavia, M.R., *A History of the LNER*, 3 vols, Allen & Unwin, London, 1983.

Bradley, D.L., *Locomotives of the Southern Railway*, 2 vols, The Railway Correspondence & Travel Society, 1977.

Bryan, T., *All in a Day's Work – Life on the GWR*, Ian Allan, London, 2004.

Christiansen, R., *A Regional History of the Railways of Great Britain: Volume VII – The West Midlands*, David & Charles, Newton Abbot.

Course, E., *The Railways of Southern England: The Main Lines*, Batsford, London, 1973.

Course, E., *The Railways of Southern England: Secondary and Branch Lines*, Batsford, London, 1974.

Crump, N., *By Rail to Victory: The story of the LNER in Wartime*, London & North Eastern Railway, London, 1947.

Darwin, B., *War on the Line, The Story of the Southern Railway in War-Time, including D-Day on the Southern*, Southern Railway, London, 1946.

Dendy Marshall, C.F., *A History of the Southern Railway*, Southern Railway Company, London, 1936.

Dixon, N., *Yorkshire Locoman – LNER Memories*, Bradford Barton, Truro, 1983.

Elliot, Sir J., *On and Off the Rails*, Allen & Unwin, London, 1982.

Fiennes, G., *I Tried to Run a Railway*, Ian Allan, London, 1967.

Glover, J., *London's Underground*, Ian Allan, London, 1999.

Gordon, D.I., *A Regional History of the Railways of Great Britain: Volume VI – The Eastern Counties*, David & Charles, Newton Abbot.

Gould, D., *Bulleid's Steam Passenger Stock*, The Oakwood Press, Salisbury, 1980

Gould, D., *Maunsell's Steam Passenger Stock, 1923–1939*, The Oakwood Press, Salisbury, 1978.

Gourvish, T., *British Railways 1948–73*, Cambridge University Press, 1987.

Gourvish, T., *British Rail 1974–1997*, Oxford University Press, Oxford, 2002.

Hamilton E., C, *The Trains We Loved*, Allen & Unwin, London, 1947.

Haresnape, B., *Maunsell Locomotives*, Ian Allan, Shepperton, 1977.

Haresnape, B., *Bulleid Locomotives*, Ian Allan, Shepperton, 1977.

Haswell, E.G.F., *Great Western Shed Designs*, Ian Allan, London, 1969.

Hoole, K., *A Regional History of the Railways of Great Britain: Volume VI – The North East*, David & Charles, Newton Abbot.

Jackson, A.A., *London's Termini*, David & Charles, Newton Abbot, 1969.

John, E., *Timetable for Victory: A brief and popular account of the railways and railway-owned dockyards of Great Britain and Ireland during the six years' war, 1939–1945*, The British Railways, London, 1946.

Jones, R.B., *British Narrow Gauge Railways*, Adam & Charles Black, London, 1958

Joy, D., *A Regional History of the Railways of Great Britain: Volume VIII – South and West Yorkshire*, David & Charles, Newton Abbot, 1975.

Kidner, R.W., *The Southern Railway*, Oakwood Press, Salisbury, 1958 and 1974.

Klapper, C.F., *Sir Herbert Walker's Southern Railway*, Ian Allan, Shepperton, 1973.

Maggs, C.G., *The GWR Swindon to Bath Line*, Sutton, Stroud.

Moody, G.T., *Southern Electric 1909–1979*, Ian Allan, Shepperton, 1979.

Newberry, P., *The Vectis Collection: Pioneering Isle of Wight Air Services*, Waterfront, Settle, 2000.

Nash, G.G., *The LMS at War*, London Midland & Scottish Railway, London, 1946.

Neele, G.P., *Railway Reminiscences*, 1904.

Nock, O.S., *A History of the LMS*, 3 vols, Allen & Unwin, London, 1983.

Nock, O.S., *Britain's Railways at War, 1939–1945*, Ian Allan, Shepperton, 1971.

Nock, O.S., *O.S. Nock's Railway Reminiscences of the Interwar Years*, Ian Allan, London, 1980.

Nock, O.S., *Sixty Years of Western Express Running*, Ian Allan, London, 1973.

Nock, O.S., *The Great Western Railway in the Twentieth Century*, Ian Allan, London, 1971

Peacock, A.J., *The Rise And Fall Of The Railway King*, Sutton, Stroud, 1995.

Pole, F.C., *Felix J.C. Pole, His Book*, published privately 1954, re-issued by Town & Country Press, 1968.

Potts, G.C., *Bankers & Pilots – Footplate Memories*, Bradford Barton, Truro, 1984.

Smullen, I., *Taken For A Ride*, Herbert Jenkins, London 1968. Ransome-Wallis, P., *On Railways At Home and Abroad*, Spring Books, London, undated.

Robertson, K., *Signalling on the Great Western Railway*, Sutton, Stroud.

Robertson, K., *GWR Gas Turbines*, Sutton, Stroud.

Robertson, K., *Odd Corners of the GWR from the days of Steam*, Sutton, Stroud.

Robertson, K., *More Odd Corners of the GWR*, Sutton, Stroud.

Russell, J.H., *A Pictorial Record of Great Western Coaches, Part II (1903–1948)*, Oxford Publishing Company, Oxford, 1973.

Russell, J.H., *A Pictorial Record of Great Western Absorbed Engines*, Oxford Publishing Company, Oxford, 1978

Simmons, J. and Biddle, G., *The Oxford Companion to British Railway History*, Oxford University Press, Oxford, 2000.

Tavender, L., *HRMS Livery Register No. 3, LSWR and Southern*, Historical Model Railway Society.

Thomas, D.StJ., *A Regional History of the Railways of Great Britain: Volume I – The West Country*, David & Charles, Newton Abbot, 1960.

Thomas, D.StJ., *A Regional History of the Railways of Great Britain: Volume VI – Scotland*, David & Charles, Newton Abbot.

Tomkins, N.S., and Sheldon, P., *Swindon & the GWR*, Sutton, Stroud.

Townroe, S.C., *The Arthurs, Nelsons and Schools of the Southern*, Ian Allan, Shepperton, 1973

Vinter, N.S., *Railway Walks GWR & SR*, Sutton, Stroud.

White, H.P., *Regional History of the Railways of Great Britain, Volume II, Southern England*, David & Charles, Newton Abbot, 1961.

White, H.P., *A Regional History of the Railways of Great Britain: Volume III – Greater London*, David & Charles, Newton Abbot.

Wilson, R.B., *Go Great Western – A History of GWR Publicity*, David & Charles, Newton Abbot, 1970.

Winkworth, D.W., *Southern Titled Trains*, David & Charles, Newton Abbot, 1988.

Wragg, D., *The Great Western Railway Handbook 1923–1947*, Haynes, 2010.

Wragg, D., *The LMS Handbook 1923–1947*, Haynes, 2010.

Wragg, D., *The LNER Handbook 1923–1947*, Haynes, 2011.

Wragg, D., *Wartime on the Railways 1939–1945*, Sutton, 2006.

Wragg, D., *Signal Failure – Politics and Britain's Railways*, Sutton, 2004.

Wragg, D., *The Southern Railway Handbook 1923–1947*, Haynes, 2011.

Index